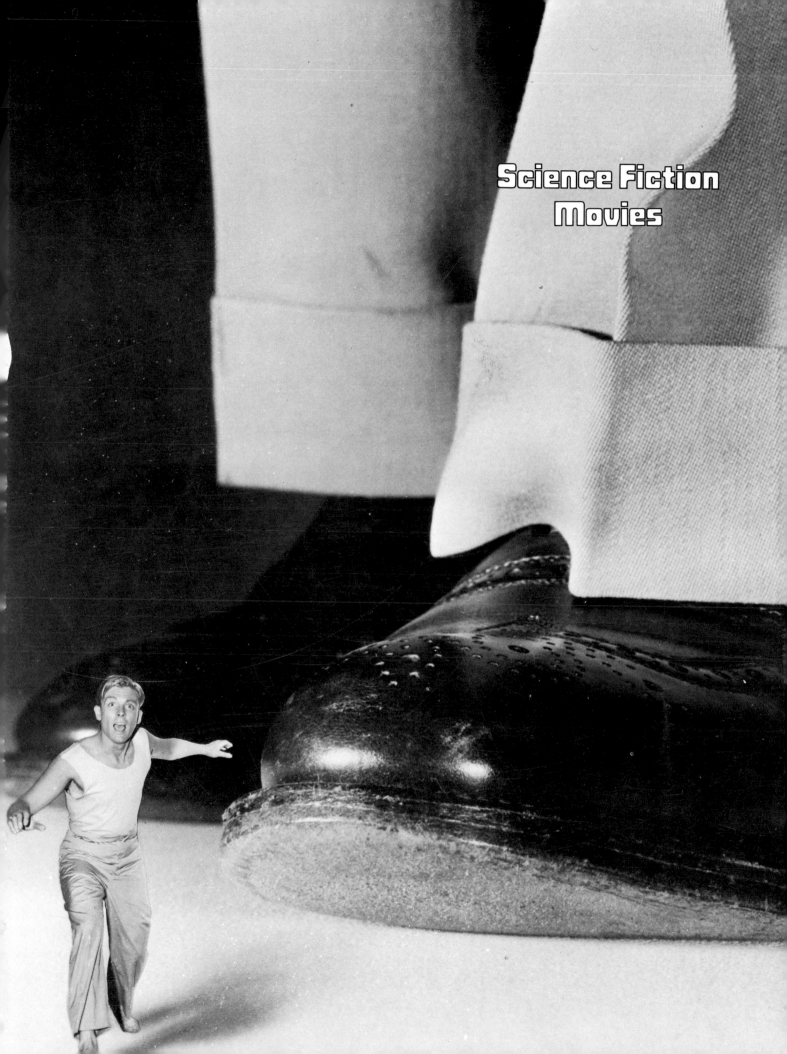

Science Fiction
Movies

# Science Fiction Movies

Gregory B. Richards

**Bison Books**

First Published in 1984 by
Bison Books Corp.
17 Sherwood Place
Greenwich, CT 06830
U.S.A.

ISBN 0 86124 099 5

Printed in Hong Kong

*To Tari, with love and thanks,*
*for making this and so much more possible*

# Contents

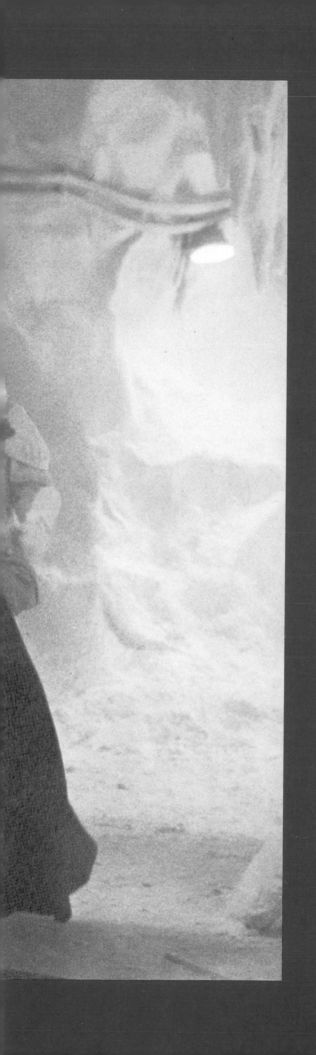

# Science and Film

*Above :* The great spaceship from *The Empire Strikes Back* (1980).
*Left :* Darth Vader, the villain of *The Empire Strikes Back*.

**S**cience fiction films represent perhaps the oldest motion picture genre—the first popular 'flicks', short and primitive as they may seem today, were science-based fantasies. Thus, it is ironic that the words 'science fiction' have such a dubious, even negative, connotation for so many people. After all, in terms of the sheer number of films that have been produced and fed to the public, science fiction and the movies, together, have been enormously popular over the years. This is remarkable considering that science fiction as a genre of literature has not been in existence much longer than the science fiction cinema.

It is interesting that when trying to locate the origin of 'science fiction' many people somehow wind up with Homer's *The Iliad* or some other ancient work of fantasy. Actually, it wasn't until the 18th century that the Age of

Reason and the Industrial Revolution reflected man's increased understanding of nature and the skills to change its course or alter its effects. These were the elements of modern thinking responsible for the birth of science fiction.

The mainstream of fiction writers has typically been slow to acknowledge the characteristics, powers, or even the existence of science. The earliest writers to do so could only reveal their awe for science, and often reacted with fear and the warning that if science were tinkered with, it would be the end of creation.

Mary Shelley best represented that trend of thought in her 1818 Gothic novel, *Frankenstein*, and for that reason her book is cited by most as the first science fiction novel. The reaction of horror toward science that her book engendered ultimately led to the horror film, but more importantly, it irreversibly linked the Gothic style with science fiction, however inappropriate.

Another author who propagated that link was Edgar Allen Poe. He is remembered mostly for his tales of the macabre and for his development of the detective story, but in fact was one of the few authors in the first half of the 19th century to so much as mention science.

Those authors who did, at the time, used science as a target for satire, not serious speculation. Poe did so in his tale, *The Unparallelled Adventures of One Hans Pfaal*, about a moon explorer. He is said to have believed that the story inspired Robert Locke Adams to publish the famous 'Moon Hoax' stories about lunar life in the *New York Sun* in 1835. Poe answered with his own satirical story in the *Sun* of 13 April 1844, 'The Balloon Hoax', a carefully contrived journal of a would-be transatlantic flight.

While Shelley and Poe and a few other authors of the period at least included science in their fiction and gave it some public appeal, Frenchman Jules Verne was to become the first widely accepted science fiction writer, beginning in the 1860s. This prolific author echoed the public's fascination for the recent developments in large-scale, long distance travel, namely, the steamship and the steam locomotive.

Verne prided himself on a 'strict' adherence to known scientific principles, though he used them only to conjure up great traveling machines and inventions that served as the instruments of expeditions, mad-scientist conquests and so forth. These were hardly the themes of a visionary such as H G Wells. In truth, Verne's extensive technical descriptions often fell short of scientific accuracy. Nonetheless, his almost maniacal love for gadgetry affected millions of readers over the years. The titles of his immensely popular works are words enough to describe the excitement he supplied to his fans: *Journey to the Center of the Earth* (1864); *Twenty Thousand Leagues Under the Sea* (1870); *Around the World in Eighty Days* (1873) and many others. The longevity of their popularity is reflected in the countless literary imitations and screen adaptations that followed.

But regarded as the father of science fiction is H G Wells,

*Opposite : A Journey to the Center of the Earth* (1959) was a stunning version of the Jules Verne story. Shown here are (left to right) Thayer David (as the villainous Count Saknussemm), James Mason, Arlene Dahl and Peter Monson as they enter a field of underground mushrooms. Pat Boone was also in the cast. But the real star of this tale of an excursion to the earth's center was the 20th Century Fox special-effects department, who developed some fascinating trick camera work and some not-to-be-believed sets.

*Below :* Captain Nemo's submarine, the *Nautilus*, under siege by native attackers, in *20,000 Leagues Under the Sea* (1954), Walt Disney's epic version of Jules Verne's nautical novel. Kirk Douglas starred as a harpooner, who, along with shipmates Peter Lorre and Paul Lukas, is plunged into a series of adventures aboard Captain Nemo's cosmic-powered sub.

an English author who had that quintessential element of the modern, serious science fiction writer lacking in Verne —a probing interest in the fundamental questions of life, the universe and the nature of human existence.

Whereas Verne was mostly preoccupied with machinery and the exploits of individuals or groups, Wells was concerned with society as a whole in much of his work. Wells probably had a better understanding of scientific principles, and more closely adhered to them, than Verne ever did. The distinction was that Wells often used inventions and technological gadgetry to help him create the setting for some fictional study of a civilization; Verne used them throughout his stories, going to great lengths to describe them and involve them in the action of his plots, typically limited in scope.

Wells was the radical of the pair, while Verne was something of a political and social conservative. The English author benefitted from an academic study of science, and had, in fact, studied under Thomas Henry Huxley, defender of Charles Darwin's theory of evolution. Wells' writings were an integral part of the social revolution that began in the late 18th century and which spawned the school of utopian theory during Wells' time. Such Wells works as *A Story of Days to Come* (1897), *When the Sleeper Wakes* (1899), *A Modern Utopia* (1905) and others of around the turn of the century, contained pessimistic views on the future of modern civilization and offered exacting projections of utopian societies.

9

Wells and Verne both lived to see the threat of technology to mankind in the form of world-wide warfare, and both were sobered by it. Verne showed some signs of distaste for machinery as his career drew to a close. One of his Nemo-type inventors, *Robur the Conqueror*, is put to death by a lightning bolt when his machinery provides him with almost godly powers—much more a religious statement about man's place than a scientific one. A villain, normally taken care of by do-gooders in other Verne works, here has overstepped mortal bounds, and only supernatural forces can snuff him out.

Wells was responsible for one of the first realistic predictions of aerial warfare in *The War in the Air*, published in 1908. The story told of an airship attack on England by Germany, and reflected many of Wells' contemporaries' views on the threat of global war.

By the early 1920s, most of the historical mileposts that would influence authors of science fiction for many years—the advent of mass transportation, the restructuring of social theory and the ever-looming capability of large-scale violence and destruction—had been passed. The pace of scientific advances led scientists, and much of the public, to believe that the universe itself was made up entirely of mechanical pieces that could be manipulated.

However, the next boom in science fiction did not indicate a turn toward fine literature. Electrical engineer and inventor Hugo Gernsback, born in Luxembourg and an emigrant to the US in 1904, was responsible for the publication of the world's first radio magazine. In it appeared a far-fetched, gadget-laden story of romance and adventure in the year 2660. It was to set the pace for pulp science fiction, and in 1926, Gernsback launched the pioneer pulp, *Amazing Stories*.

That event set off the pulp magazine era which saw both imaginative and pure hack writers' comments on everything from ray guns to atomic annihilation. The combination of a large number of fledgling publications in the 1930s and a spate of eager readers set off the big boom of the 1940s. *Astounding Science Fiction*, under editor John W Campbell, was the king of the pulps. Campbell's own contribution to science fiction was substantial; he emphasized the need for better writing and a more intelligent attitude toward engineering and how it related to mankind.

Science fiction's 'Golden Age' of publishing in the 1940s came to an abrupt end with the beginning of American involvement in World War II, when economic restrictions, including various forms of rationing, made publishing difficult. Yet the war was to help change the course of science fiction literature.

The world became witness to man's destructive capacity and to the horrible results of atomic weaponry development. No genre was better suited to discuss these themes than science fiction, which had the ability to place too-real situations at hand into perspective, on some far-off planet or in a future civilization. Here, readers could face bigger questions about themselves and society; the pain of nonfiction's 'mirror' was removed.

Many authors took up these questions in the softer sciences—psychology, sociology, anthropology. During the 50s and 60s, their work reflected new and complex themes, such as the world after nuclear war, man's future existence and a more sophisticated curiosity toward extra-terrestrial life. The sexual revolution presented the opportunity for extrapolations on the conflict between the sexes—including visions of worlds where women reigned politically and socially over men. Also, the slick commercialization of day-to-day middle-class life provoked satirical examinations of the effects of mass media advertising and the capitalist ethic.

Since then, disillusionment with government, disdain for war involvement as well as the business community and further advances in technology such as the US lunar landing have led to an even wider variety of science fiction topics. An increasing emphasis on the effects of drugs, biotechnology and genetic engineering on human evolution is seen.

Despite all of the growing sophistication of science fiction, there are still millions of readers and viewers of 'comic strip' style science fiction, replete with awesome aliens, ray guns and matter/anti-matter spaceships. It is the variety of literature that first inspired the dreaded term, 'sci-fi.' Its sound is as suggestive of fads and hype as the word 'hi-fi' was during the 50s.

But this is one of the unusual characteristics of science fiction: a sometimes incredible tendency to inspire fanatic, cult-like followings. With all due respect to intelligent science fiction and its unparalleled power of addressing questions of stellar magnitude, we must conclude that many cling to the genre like some favorite old toy.

Feverish trading, collection and worship of tattered old pulp magazines, stills from low-grade 'B' pictures and, more recently, such paraphernalia as 'Mr. Spock ears' have a lot to say about science fiction. It has always appealed, since Verne's works became best-sellers, to juveniles. The space opera, after all, has as much action as a ten-year-old can stand. And for one of the genre's key consumers, the teenage male, two desirable but seemingly unreachable goals, travel to a place far from home and the companionship of a pretty girl, are conveniently linked in the plot of most 'B' movies and pulps.

*Top left:* The mother ship comes to earth in *Close Encounters of the Third Kind* (1977). The picture tells the story of a small spacecraft and then of its mother ship, and the first communication between earthlings and extraterrestrials. In this landing sequence the mammoth ship fills the screen and leaves the audience as awestruck as the actors.
*Left: Star Trek—The Motion Picture* (1979), a film drawn from the television series, was a financial success, but it was criticized as being no more than a television episode stretched out to a full-length feature. Starring were three of the members of the original TV cast. Left to right: Leonard Nimoy as the emotionless Mr Spock; William Shatner as Admiral (formerly Captain) James Kirk: DeForest Kelley as the irascible Dr 'Bones' McCoy.

One of the most delightful aspects of science fiction is that it invites young imaginations to reach toward the stars and ponder things more important than gunfights between good guys and bad. So delightful is the experience that when science fiction fans grow up, they often take with them a nostalgic affection for the genre's more simple-minded forms. This is true even when they learn to appreciate fine science fiction literature. No other type of film or literature creates the same sort or degree of response among its followers.

Various historic events and periods have sparked evolutionary movements in science fiction literature. Similarly, such events during the 20th century can be cited for helping to create public acceptance, and at times, rejection of the science fiction film.

For instance, the threat of German violence and domination during the cinema's pre-World War I years created something of a phobia of invasion, and films dealing with technological warfare and destruction became popular. But the war came soon enough, and there was a sudden lack of interest in large-scale violence on the screen.

The same attitude prevailed during the isolationist 1920s. People favored the recently developed horror film, born in Germany, whose film-makers were translating the pain and somber mood of their defeated nation to celluloid. The trend began with Otto Rippert's *Homunculus*, one of the first dramas about an artificial human being, and Robert Wiene's *The Cabinet of Dr Caligari*, a tale of a mad scientist and his pet homicidal freak. The 'science' in such films was limited to a laboratory setting or some sort of small expedi-

*Above :* A moment of gaiety in *Metropolis* (1926), Fritz Lang's towering film about a city of the 21st century.

*Opposite top :* In *Forbidden Planet* (1957) the team of astronauts lands on Altair Four. The film was one of the few science-fiction romps to win special acclaim as a lively futuristic comic strip. The tame robot, Robby, in this film later went on to star in *The Invisible Boy* (1957), and the 1960s series on television, *Lost in Space*.

*Opposite :* The evil Dr Caligari (Werner Krauss) awakens his somnambulist, Cesare (Conrad Veidt). The scene is inside an exhibition tent at a carnival in *The Cabinet of Dr Caligari* (1919).

tion. The result of scientific tinkering most often posed hazards to individuals or limited groups, but not society.

That remained the case until after World War II, although a few land-mark films, such as Fritz Lang's *Metropolis*, a statement about social stratification, and William Cameron Menzies' *Things to Come*, which discussed H G Wells' vision of future civilization, were welcome exceptions.

But with World War II came the V-2 rocket and the atomic bomb. Popular fear of nuclear warfare and anxiety over international relations were reflected in a new on-slaught of science fiction films. Hollywood used atomic radiation as a convenient device to turn normal animals into enormous, population-threatening pests, bring prehistoric creatures back to life, and make men shrink or enlarge on cue. The 'B' movies' 'Golden Age', if it can be called that, was under way, and nothing could stop it.

A few well-meaning films brought serious science fiction before the public; George Pal's *Destination Moon*, for instance, helped to make space travel believable to the non-scientific community. Other science fiction films, though aimed at exploiting the 'sci-fi' cinema boom, some-how retained the creative talents of their writers and directors. Though audiences may not have known it, some films were endowed with lasting quality and some startling, sensitive messages, including Robert Wise's political *The Day the Earth Stood Still*; Don Siegel's slick classic, *The Invasion of the Body Snatchers*, an underground favorite since and Fred MacLeod Wilcox's thoughtful *Forbidden Planet*. By 1959, well-known directors of other film genres

lent some respectability to the science fiction cinema, notably with Stanley Kramer's strongly anti-war *On the Beach*, which also featured an impressive all-star cast.

On the whole, the horror and monster movies that were inspired by science fiction films brought to the public a misleading idea of what science fiction was. The problem remains today, perhaps as Godzilla's legacy to the cultural world. But the 1960s brought several intelligent science fiction films, two of which, 1964's *Dr. Strangelove* and 1968's momentuous *2001: A Space Odyssey*, were the work of Stanley Kubrick. *Dr. Strangelove* is noted as one of the first satirical films of the genre, which received the sort of critical acclaim (and controversy, at that) new to science fiction films.

Social upheaval during the decade, including the struggle for civil rights and mass anti-war protests, prepared audiences for films taking cracks at the government and at the business establishment, including Francois Truffaut's *Fahrenheit 451* in 1966, about a future society where books are banned entirely. Government has disposed with the inconsistency of freedom of speech.

The same variety of themes continued into the 70s, and Hollywood began placing more trust in legitimate science fiction writers. It was rewarded with the success of films such as Robert Wise's *The Andromeda Strain*, based on the novel by Michael Crichton, which relied heavily on scientific realism for the success of its plot and theme.

Perhaps the most significant turning point in the science fiction cinema since has been its mass-popularization, beginning with George Lucas' romping *Star Wars*. That film's incredible earnings inspired Hollywood producers to invest heavily in science fiction movies, and the last few years have seen not only a large number of entries to the genre, but also highly sophisticated special effects and a few intelligent story lines.

Sadly, Hollywood's ability to completely bungle a good science fiction concept was brought to a new pinnacle. Producers frantic to cash in on the boom were responsible for aesthetic failures such as *Star Trek: The Motion Picture* and Disney's *The Black Hole*, both released with much fanfare in 1979.

But if ever there will be a time for a new movement in

*Top*: The air stewardess enters the cockpit area of the spacecraft *Aries* to serve a meal to the crew on duty. *2001: A Space Odyssey* (1968), Stanley Kubrick's masterpiece.
*Left*: Arthur Hill and James Olson flee by racing through a corridor when an alarm sounds in *The Andromeda Strain* (1971).
*Opposite top*: Stanley Kubrick constructed a realistic war room for his production of *Dr Strangelove or How I Learned to Stop Worrying and Love the Bomb* (1963).
*Opposite bottom*: In *The Andromeda Strain* (1971), scientist James Olson quickly gets out of his anti-contamination suit to deal with a lethal organism from outer space as Paula Kelly and George Mitchell watch warily.

*Above :* In *The Incredible Shrinking Man* (1957) Grant Williams has shrunk to a point where he needs the help of what to him is a giant pencil to save himself from disappearing into a storm sewer. He played a scientist who, on being exposed to radiation, begins to decrease in size, continually diminishing until he ends as a molecule within a molecule. The picture is memorable for the special effects that are genuinely frightening, especially when he has to hide from a cat and fight off a giant spider.

*Opposite :* Star Wars (1977) was the hit of the year. It was described as 'a phantasmagoric space-opera, an intergalactic nine-million-dollar fairy tale . . . and one of the most technically dazzling and enjoyable movies since the art form was invented.' Here Luke Skywalker (Mark Hamill) lectures the two lovable robots, C3PO (the tall one) and R2D2.

science fiction films, it is now. Science fiction equals box-office cash, as far as producers are concerned. Two sequels to *Star Trek : The Motion Picture* have appeared, as well as further installments in the *Star Wars* series. Certainly, top producers will continue to seek science fiction properties. Perhaps they will resist robbing them of the science fiction content, and realize that the public is learning what science fiction really is, and what it is not.

But an economic movement in the motion picture industry may also aid these films. More and more independent producers are becoming capable of supporting ventures discarded by the major studios. Filmmakers such as George Lucas and Francis Ford Coppola built their own film empires without the aid of traditional Hollywood backing. In that 'magic' city, that development has sent home a hard message.

Audiences are beginning to see that science fiction films are not all 'monster trash' as most were during the 50s. Monster films, horror films and science fiction films are all branches of fantasy—creations based on the mind's imagination.

What sets science fiction apart from the other genres is that it suggests changes in man's environment, man himself (physical, mental, social) and the universe as we know it; importantly, it proposes that these changes have some rational explanation, regardless of whether one is provided.

These changes may be in the form of mental transformations, such as the stimulation of intelligence seen in *Charly* of 1968, the story of a mentally retarded person who is made a temporary genius through the use of drugs. They may be in the form of physical changes, *The Incredible Shrinking Man* of 1957 being an obvious example.

The changes may occur in man's environment, whether in the form of a natural or man-made catastrophe, caused by some manipulation of natural laws, including nuclear warfare.

But very frequently in science fiction, the changes suggested are displacements in time or space, including views of the future or the prehistoric ages; visits from aliens, friendly or otherwise; expeditions to other stars or planets.

Many people mistakenly assume that science fiction must involve some sort of scientific hardware or high technology, but these films often observe biological, psychological, sociological and many other types of changes. Often, the most effective science fiction involves neither futuristic space travel nor fantastic inventions, but concentrates on the interaction of people in a subtly altered environment.

Now that we have traced science fiction's roots, discussed its translation to the screen, and better defined it, we can take a closer look at those films which are part of its history. Of course, a book of this size could not begin to describe, or even list, all of the science fiction films ever made. Subjectively chosen are films which have made a distinct mark on the genre, whether the film was good or bad, enjoyable or offensive, successful or an overnight failure.

# The Silent Films

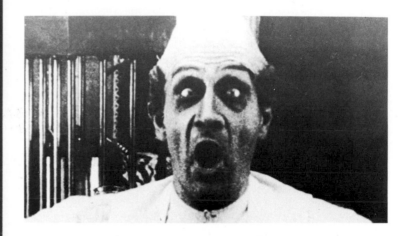

*Above :* The insane scientist in *The Madness of Dr Tube* (1914).
*Opposite :* Shooting a robot scene in *Metropolis* (1926).

cholars of cinema do not always agree naming the first science fiction film, although it is recognized that the birth of the motion picture and of the science fiction genre occurred almost simultaneously. The man credited by most with sparking the growth of science fiction films, however, is Georges Méliès. A Parisian artist and magician fascinated with entertaining audiences through illusion, Méliès witnessed in 1895 a demonstration of moving pictures by film pioneers Auguste and Louis Lumière in Paris.

Méliès was so taken by the almost mystical effect of these first 'movies' on audiences that he at once attempted to buy the Lumière brothers' equipment. The Lumières, already reaping handsome profits from their invention, refused to sell. But Méliès eventually obtained a projector invented by English film pioneer Robert Paul and found a way to alter the device to record pictures. By 1897, Méliès had stumbled upon the genesis of the science fiction cinema: the camera could be made to lie.

Méliès' specialty was trick effects—he is credited, for instance, with inventing stop-motion photography, used to make objects seem to 'disappear' on film. Multiple exposures, slow and fast motion, fades and dissolves can all be attributed to Méliès' early efforts. But because his career had been devoted to stage theatrics, Méliès' films never took on an entirely believable tone—he was a master of caricature, of startling tricks.

Borrowing from his discoveries, the Lumière brothers produced a fanciful short in 1897 called *La Charcuterie Mècanique (The Sausage Machine)* in which pigs are seen walking into a complicated-looking device and popping out as link sausages. This simple bit of fantasy was probably the first science fiction footage produced and it inspired a great many imitations in following years.

George Smith, a British filmmaker, added cats, ducks, even overshoes in his *Making Sausages*, 1897; Biograph's *The Sausage Machine* converted dogs into sausage. The idea was probably fully milked by the time Thomas Edison himself, the father of American film, with his director Edwin S Porter, produced *Fun In a Butcher Shop* in 1901. Here, more dogs were turned into sausage. If only for variety, the duo reversed the tried-and-true formula in 1904's *The Dog Factory*—you guessed right, with sausages turning into dogs! That Porter could possibly be responsible for the seminal Western *The Great Train Robbery* seems miraculous!

But audiences' tastes did become more sophisticated, for in 1902 what is regarded by many as the first true science fiction film was created by Georges Méliès. *A Trip to the Moon*, released as *Le Voyage Dans La Lune*, borrowed heavily from H G Wells' novel *The First Men in the Moon*, published the year before, and Jules Verne's *From Earth to the Moon*, already 40 years in print. Méliès' film tells of a pompous scientific society's plans to explore the Moon. A few brave souls are selected for the space flight, which consists of being hurled at the Moon from a giant 'space gun', in the comforts of a huge metal shell. After landing squarely in the eye of the Man in the Moon, the travelers participate in a variety of comic sketches designed to show off director Méliès' bag of cinematic tricks.

The travelers crawl through craters, witness a volcanic eruption, experience −40°F chills and bump into an unfriendly lot of cardboard creatures resembling giant lobsters, patterned after Wells' Selenites. After battling the feisty crustaceans, the would-be astronauts make their escape back to Earth, where they are received with great parades and decorations from the authorities.

While we might consider their accomplishment ques-

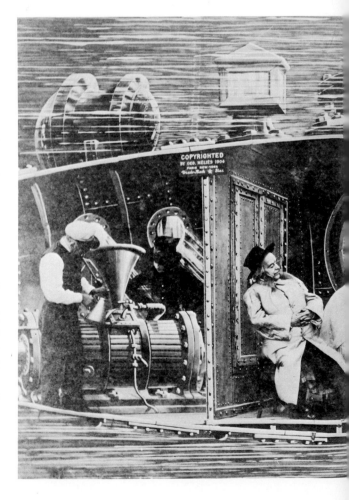

*Top right :* The train is airborne in Georges Méliès' *The Impossible Voyage* (1904). Note the submarine in the last car.

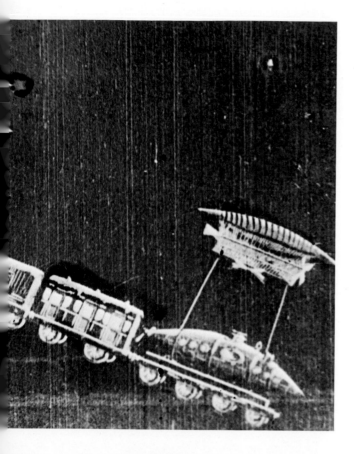

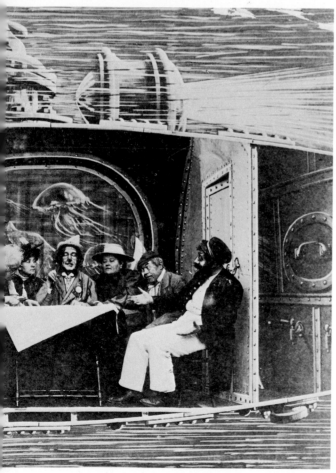

tionable, the film was a great financial success. Though its actors were chorus girls and singers borrowed from local clubs and theaters, the film presented audiences with a fantastic vision of the possible. In the form of a comic revue, *A Trip to the Moon* provides in its 14 minutes the cinema's first dramatic presentation of space travel.

Méliès' film was both pirated and copied in Great Britain and the United States, and a variety of films portraying trips to the Moon, Mars, Jupiter and elsewhere followed in the early 1900s. Méliès himself, whose Star Film Company catalogue boasted some 400 titles already, went on to produce such films as *Le Voyage a Travers l'Impossible (The Impossible Voyage)*, 1904. The film was a re-working of *A Trip to the Moon*'s basic plot with the addition of a preposterous flying train for a vehicle.

Perhaps a more significant film was Walter Booth's 1909 *The Airship Destroyer*. Booth, a magician and artist like Méliès, directed a number of films involving one of the most exciting scientific developments of his time—the invention of the airplane. Booth was no doubt influenced by Wells' popular novel *The War In The Air*, laced with predictions of aerial bombardment, published in 1908. Booth's film, released in the United States as *The Battle in the Clouds* in 1910, stands out not because of its realistic effects depicting aerial warfare, but because it was the first genuinely serious science fiction film. Prior to its release, films in the genre more often than not leaned on camera tricks and fantasy, not science, to support a story.

*The Airship Destroyer* is also important because it reflected growing acceptance of the possible effects of scientific advances, however gruesome. In the story, England is attacked by German airships, and when all defenses fail, a young inventor resorts to his own ultimate weapon—a radio-controlled torpedo. The enemy is wiped out, England is saved, and our hero even rescues his girl— and a new plot formula has been etched on the face of the science fiction film that will be used again and again.

Booth's film was a great success and a flurry of serialized sequels and imitations followed. Foreign invasion was a hot topic for Europeans, whose paranoia over the increasing German threat was ignited by science fiction films. When World War I broke out in 1914, Americans' fear of involvement in the bloodshed kindled interest in a number of films dealing with invasion. Even the great D W Griffith, who was ultimately responsible for defining the modern film, contributed to the trend with his 1916 remake of *The Airship Destroyer*, entitled *The Flying Torpedo*.

In the face of more sophisticated themes and special effects, the films of Méliès and others, based on poking fun at 'those crazy scientists' and their machines, could not compete for the filmgoer's attention, and gradually faded in popularity.

*Bottom left:* An interior view of the submarine being pulled by the flying train in *The Impossible Voyage* (1904).

21

By the second decade of the century, most of the common themes of the science fiction film had been established. Besides many film renditions of Verne's and Wells' popular works, many serials and feature-length films had explored high-technology warfare, Earth's prehistoric development and visions of the future. Two other important films helped to establish another genre based on science fiction—horror films.

French filmmaker Abel Gance, picking up France's science fiction cinema where Méliès left off, directed 1914's *La Folie du Docteur Tube (The Madness of Doctor Tube)*, an experimental short film about a scientist gone insane as the result of tinkering with light waves. The film presents striking visual effects using distorted lenses, mirrors and other camera tricks. More importantly, Gance created the first 'mad scientist'—that creature who would go on to become the venerable stand-by of horror films.

Otto Rippert created a serial in 1916 that is said to be a major contributor to the evolution of the science fiction thriller, made in Germany. That country would dominate science fiction films for the remainder of the silent era. Borrowing from Mary Shelley's novel, *Frankenstein*, Rippert's six-part series was called *Homunkulus der Führer (Homunculus the Leader)*, and featured an artificial human created by a scientist and his faithful assistant. When the handsome, good-willed creature discovers his origins, he feels rejected, and—through the remaining five installments—wreaks every type of havoc imaginable on mankind. Only the gods themselves are finally able to put a stop to the rampage, destroying Homunculus with a bolt of lightning.

Many feel that one of the classics of the decade, and the progenitor of the modern horror film, *The Cabinet of Dr Caligari*, is owing in large part to *Homunculus*. Robert Wiene directed this 1919 German film which tells of a mad scientist's carnival attraction, a somnambulist, or sleepwalker. Caligari's creature, between performances, moonlights as a homicidal maniac for his master. The film is not really science fiction, but it is important for three reasons.

First, *Caligari*'s unprecedented level of terror and moody suspense laid the path for creators of horror films in years to come. Also, the film's highly stylized settings, reminiscent of Cubist modern art, revolutionized the use of art to create different moods on film. Finally, it brought together the talents of director Wiene, the UFA studio, and a scriptwriter named Fritz Lang. That combination would go on to create the first science fiction masterpiece, *Metropolis*, in 1926.

It is important to understand why Germany came to lead the science fiction film industry during the post-war

*Above*: John Frederson broods about his 21st-century city in *Metropolis*, Fritz Lang's science-fiction film of 1926.
*Right*: Caligari smirks as his somnambulist, Cesare, is examined in *The Cabinet of Dr Caligari* (1919).
*Opposite top*: A view of the heart of the city from *Metropolis*. Fritz Lang received his inspiration on a trip to New York.

years. The German people had been crushed both spiritually and financially as the result of defeat at the hands of the Allied Powers, and German filmmakers naturally reflected a somber national attitude in their creations. Crime, tyranny, torture and death figured prominently in film after film. This emphasis on visualizing the morose was responsible for much experimentation with special effects and themes, revitalizing the science fiction film.

Lang, inspired by a visit to post-war New York City, was fascinated with the future. Formerly a student of architecture, Lang wanted to express on film his vision of future cities, and at the same time issue a caution to audiences about human nature. Working with a script written by his wife, Thea von Harbou, and collaborating with Robert Wiene and UFA producer Erich Pommer, Lang directed a classic epic melodrama set in the year 2000 AD.

*Metropolis* suffers from a somewhat complicated plot. The giant city, ruled by an industrialist named John Frederson, is divided sharply into two social classes, the ruling aristocracy and the enslaved working class. The son of the Master of Metropolis, Freder, becomes curious about the underground working class he has heard about, and after a glimpse of a beautiful poor girl named Maria, steals away to learn more about the city's dark secret. Below ground, he is horrified by the tortured existence of the workers who tend the city's machinery—and moved by Maria's message to her people that mediation between labor and management must be sought.

The city ruler, Frederson, however, acts to stifle the seeds of revolution and commissions a mad scientist to construct a robot replica of Maria to confuse and disorganize the workers. The scene where the mad scientist, Rotwang, brings Maria's double to life is one of the most powerful creation scenes ever devised for a science fiction film.

Something goes wrong with Frederson's plans, however. The robot incites the workers to riot and destroy the city's machinery and waterworks. The workers' homes are flooded, and the rioting workers attempt to burn the robot at the stake. Only the real Maria's last minute escape from Rotwang and the rescue of the workers' children from the floodwaters prevent total catastrophe. Freder saves Maria from a menacing Rotwang, and the two reveal the fake Maria, calm the workers and reconcile with Frederson. The Master of Metropolis, happily, realizes that 'the heart must mediate between the brain and the hands', and the film ends with a handshake between Frederson and the workers' foreman. Everyone looks on elatedly, perhaps forgetting about the mess they'll have to mop up with overtime hours.

While *Metropolis* suffers from an absurd storyline, it remains a strikingly original vision of the future city. Its powerful architecture, conveyed through brilliant special effects and detailed model work, impressed even those critics who found the story lame or boring. The film's visual style was to have an effect on every cinematic portrayal of the future for years to come.

23

Revolution was also a particularly relevant topic for a Russian film called *Aelita: The Revolt of the Robots*, directed by Yakov Protazanov in 1924. Based on a novel written by Alexei Tolstoy, the film tells the story of two Russian cosmonauts who visit Mars by spaceship. They discover a world caught up in a class war between a ruling aristocracy and the working class, as in *Metropolis*. The film serves as an outlet for propaganda about Communist doctrines (as our heroes lead the workers to revolt). Like *Metropolis*, many felt *Aelita* had a silly plot, but it has remarkable Cubist sets, grotesque costuming and some well-directed group scenes to recommend it as one of the better science fiction films of the 1920s.

Not to be overlooked is an interesting film made in the United States by director Harry Hoyt. *The Lost World*, released by First National in 1925, was based on the 1912 novel by Arthur Conan Doyle, and featured a cast including Wallace Beery, Bessie Love and Lewis Stone. In the film, an expedition to South America is caught up in a number of adventures, including an attack by a superhuman ape-man and the capture of a brontosaurus. Trouble erupts when the bronto breaks out of its shackles in London during an exhibition and begins smashing buildings. When it attempts to cross Tower Bridge, it falls into the River Thames, swims out to sea and is never seen again.

*The Lost World* is notable because of its extensive dinosaur model work. Though Edward S Porter and Stuart Blackton had used stop-motion animation as early as 1906 to animate objects, Harry Hoyt's film was the first to use sophisticated models and superimposition techniques to place both scurrying humans and dinosaurs on the screen simultaneously. Willis O'Brien and Marcel Delgado used

*Top :* The beautiful queen, Aelita, strolling through her palace in the USSR's science-fiction film *Aelita* (1924). It was a story of two young Russians who visit Mars and encounter the beautiful queen. One falls in love with Aelita while the other leads the planet's slave population in a revolt against her totalitarian rule—a theme that science fiction films would use repeatedly through the years—social injustice.

*Right :* The giant ape, Kong, carries the beautiful Fay Wray to the top of the Empire State Building in New York (she is on the ledge) and fights off the Army Air Corps fighters that have come to shoot him down in *King Kong* (1933). The true star of the picture was a model ape created by special-effects wizard Willis O'Brien. The doll, standing about two feet tall, was animated by photographing him a frame at a time against a background of miniature sets.

*Opposite top :* The rocket ship in Fritz Lang's *Die Frau im Monde (The Girl in the Moon)*, released in 1929. The design of spacecraft in the movies did not change much for the next *30* years or more.

almost 50 miniature dinosaurs to create the animated effects—and both went on to create the convincing *King Kong* of 1933.

What the significant films of the mid-1920s share is a heretofore unseen commitment to quality and realism in the science fiction film. In both *Metropolis* and *Aelita*, for instance, many thousands of extras were used to fill the screen during crowd action scenes; both films are noted for their effective management of such large-scale throngs. Technical innovations such as the matté technique of superimposition, superior model work and camera-produced effects added to the sophistication of the science fiction film, and hence its widespread popular acceptance.

Fritz Lang attempted to infuse the same level of quality the studio UFA was known for in his last silent science fiction film made there, *Die Frau im Mond (The Woman in the Moon)*. Again, Lang's wife, Thea von Harbou, collaborated on the script about a space trip to the Moon in search of gold resources. The travelers in the film discover their treasure but struggle among themselves over it, damaging their spacecraft. The flight engineer and his girl friend must remain behind so that the others may return, hoping that they may some day be rescued.

As in *Metropolis*, the special effects, including a spectacular rocket launch scene, help overshadow a melodramatic plot and several scientific inconsistencies in the author's concept of space travel. But the film is nonetheless memorable as the last of the major silent science fiction films. Surprisingly, Lang had the opportunity to add mechanically recorded speech and sound effects to *Die Frau im Mond*, but he declined to do so.

# The Sound Films

*Opposite :* A scene from *Slaughterhouse-Five* (1972).
*Above :* The mothership approaches: *Close Encounters* (1977).

The advent of sound in the motion picture industry presented seemingly unlimited opportunities for creators of science fiction films better to relate complex plots and ideas to their audiences. Ironically, the huge success of *Frankenstein* and *Dracula* for Universal in 1931 created a horror film movement that was to eclipse any significant development in science fiction films during the 1930s. These horror films, directed by James Whale and Tod Browning, and starring Boris Karloff, Bela Lugosi and others, put to use all of the long-developed characteristics of the German horror film. The result was an American public that wanted even more terror than the Hollywood studios could pump out.

Though science fiction's growth during the 1930s was limited mostly to pulp magazines, it is reassuring to know that the decade saw a few important films that maintained audience interest. Furthermore, the science fiction serial was born, feeding space adventure to millions of children who would someday be able to appreciate a renaissance in futuristic films.

1930 brought about *Just Imagine*, the first science fiction comedy-musical. This lavish David Butler film starred John Garrick and Maureen O'Sullivan in a story about a 1980 couple who want to get married but are prevented from doing so by society. To prove himself worthy, the young man agrees to test a spaceship on a flight to Mars; joining him is a sidekick played by vaudeville comedian El Brendel, a man from 1930 who has just been reawakened and is discovering the marvels of the future.

In a series of ridiculous adventures, the heroes make jokes over what man has come to (babies from vending machines, pills for bourbon and steak, and flying automobiles similar to helicopters in every garage). At every revelation, we hear El Brendel sigh to the audience, 'Ah, give me the *good* old days!' and disappointingly, this is about all the film has to say. However, some fascinating views of New York, reminiscent of *Metropolis*, and a few spaceship effects make the film interesting to see.

Two films based on H G Wells novels provided the more serious science fiction fan with a little subsistence during the decade's first three years. Based on Wells' 1896 *The Island of Dr Moreau*, Paramount's 1932 *The Island of Lost Souls* has much to recommend it, including an effective blend of science fiction and horror by director Erle Kenton and a masterful performance by Charles Laughton as Dr Moreau. Playing an evil (but not mad) scientist who attempts to transform mammals into men with crude and barbaric surgical methods, Laughton instills the role with the same evil he gave to Captain Bligh in *Mutiny On the Bounty*. His cruel, whip-cracking character, along with effective creature effects and a ghoulish climax, make the film a favorite of science fiction fans.

Unfortunately, Wells himself was disappointed with the film—perhaps because of the negative reaction of his native England and of New Zealand and a few American states, which banned the film.

However, Wells was more appreciative of the film version of his 1897 tale, *The Invisible Man*. The 1933 Universal film was directed by *Frankenstein*'s James Whale with an unusual mixture of horror, straight up, and black humor. Critics were divided in their comments about the direction, but the special effects by John P Fulton received praise from all. Claude Rains, as the man who is in search of an antidote to a drug which has rendered him invisible, gives an effective performance as his character goes insane and sets out for revenge on mankind. Considering we see Rains in only a few scenes of the film, his performance is even more admirable.

Also at a height of technical quality, though lacking in as much excitement, were several science fiction films from Germany. 1932's *FP 1 Does Not Answer (FP 1 Antwortet Nicht)*, directed by Karl Hartl, offers outstanding visual

*Above:* A set showing the city of New York in the year 1980, from *Just Imagine* (1930). New Yorkers of the 1980s all have numbers instead of names and they also have their own airplanes.

*Opposite top left:* Charles Laughton disciplines his human animal monsters in *The Island of Lost Souls* (1932). The creature with the most hair is Bela Lugosi. The film was an adaptation of H G Wells' novel *The Island of Dr Moreau*.

*Opposite top right:* Gloria Stuart looks aghast as she learns that her boy friend, Claude Rains (behind the bandages), is invisible, in *The Invisible Man* (1933). The picture made a star of Rains although his face was seen only briefly, in death.

*Right:* An action scene on the platform in *FP 1 Does Not Answer (FP 1 Antwortet Nicht)*, released in 1932.

effects but a storyline that critics called slow-moving and weak-plotted. The film concerns the construction of a giant mid-Atlantic landing platform for long-distance airplane flights, and a love triangle between the builders' sister and the project's creators. Though the story leaves something to be desired, some interesting models of the huge platform at sea are seen. Also interesting is the fact that the film was shot with three different casts, English, French and German, for international release.

Another German film concerned with linking Europe with the United States was also released in German, French and English. *Der Tunnel*, 1933, was released in English as *The TransAtlantic Tunnel* in 1935. Like *FP 1 Does Not Answer*, *Tunnel* is a wholly technological story, the object of which, a project to better international relations, runs into various snags and attempts at sabotage along the way. Some believe that these films reflected the thoughts of German filmmakers, who, feeling the pressures of censorship from the Nazi regime, would soon be fleeing to Hollywood.

While most of the popular horror films of the 30s made use of various science fiction conventions to kick-off the plot, which then basically centered on homicidal rampage or mass hysteria, one film can be included in the science fiction genre because of its increased emphasis on the effects of technology—especially when that technology is mishandled.

*The Invisible Ray*, 1936, directed for Universal by Lambert Hillyer, starred both great actors of the horror films, Boris Karloff and Bela Lugosi. Karloff plays a mad scientist who believes that a meteorite containing a highly powerful radioactive substance landed in Africa hundreds of years ago. He and a colleague (Lugosi) form an expedition to find the substance, and ultimately the scientist, alone in a volcanic crater, discovers the object. However, he becomes contaminated by it—his hands and face glow with radioactivity, and his fingers impart the touch of death. Also poisoned in his thoughts, Karloff believes that his colleagues are conspiring to steal his discovery and goes about murdering them. Only his mother, by depriving him of his antidote drugs, can stop him, and the scientist dies flaming with radioactivity.

John P Fulton, who had created the effects for *The Invisible Man*, again provided excellent illusions, especially during the film's prehistoric scenes where the meteorite plummets to Earth. Karloff would repeat many times his role of good-willed scientist gone mad as the result of some discovery, in a number of Hollywood films.

The most-remembered science fiction film of the decade, however, came not from Hollywood but from Great Britain, and had the prestigious distinction of being written for the screen by none other than H G Wells.

Wells was already in his 70s by the time Alexander Korda, a highly successful Hungarian-born producer during England's cinematic boom of the 30s, convinced him that Wells' novel, *The Shape of Things to Come*, was ideal movie material. When Wells agreed to write the screenplay,

*Top :* The man in the suit is Boris Karloff in *The Invisible Ray* (1936). He is a scientist who develops a touch of death.

Korda was accepting the risk that the author might not be capable of producing usable material—indeed, he tactfully rejected the first draft and called in scriptwriter Lajos Biro for assistance. Wells' 1933 non-fiction work, like most of his later works, was more of a pompous, polemical essay on the nature of social forces, but after several drafts a plot line was established.

*Things To Come*, directed by William Cameron Menzies and released in 1936, tells the story of civilization through three time periods. Everytown (which bears a resemblance to London) in 1940 is home to John Cabal (Raymond Massey) and his family, who are in the midst of celebrating Christmas when the sound of air raid sirens fills the air. World War II has been declared, and through a lengthy montage of high-technology warfare scenes we see the destruction of Everytown and the conversion of the world into a barbaric wasteland.

By 1966, there are no more resources for war, and a plague of the 'Wandering Sickness' persists. Everytown is a pile of rubble, and its inhabitants scurry about battling the 'hill people' for commodities. Suddenly, from the air, appears John Cabal, complete with four-foot-high helmet, in a strange aircraft. Cabal warns the citizens of Everytown that the fighting must come to an end, and identifies himself as a member of a peaceful scientific group dedicated to rebuilding civilization. The Boss of Everytown (Ralph Richardson), a gruff, mobster-like militarist, ignores Cabal's message and instead tries to force him to help improve his air forces; when Cabal refuses, he is thrown into jail. But soon his fellow pilots appear in their futuristic aircraft, blanketing the area with 'peace gas' and beginning a period of reconstruction. Again, a montage of scenes is used to propel the viewer into the future, depicting gigantic semi-automatic construction machines at work. We arrive at the year 2036, and Everytown has been converted into a Wellsian utopia, a gleaming white city resembling a cross between Lang's *Metropolis* and the most confusing of freeway interchanges.

The only conflict in this otherwise antiseptic never-never land is between the scientists, led by John Cabal's grandson Oswald (also played by Raymond Massey) and a group of artistic humanists, led by Theotocopulos (Sir Cedric Hardwicke), who feel that science has gone a step too far: they are about to blast Cabal's daughter and her fiancé to the moon. A mob attempts to prevent the firing of the giant space gun (embarrassingly reminiscent of the one in *A Trip to the Moon*), but the scientists are able to launch the capsule anyway. Oswald Cabal stares knowingly after the craft and states, 'We can remain animals or we can grow and evolve. All the universe—or nothingness. Which shall it be?'

The answer is perhaps a bit too obvious at the end of a film which some have criticized for its naive, almost fascist idealism—after all, the film supports the theory that a select group can best judge the course of human destiny, disregarding free speech and the democratic process. The film itself has other flaws—wooden acting (except on the

*Above:* Raymond Massey (in white) played several roles in the H G Wells' fantasy *Things to Come* (1936).

part of Richardson), a meandering script and some shameful scientific errors, such as the 'space gun'. Many of the special effects, supervised by Ned Mann and created by a team of imported Hollywood effects wizards, are ineffective, though for the most part they helped to create a stunning visual story. Once again, a science fiction film's cinematic effects, as opposed to its plot or theme, had stolen the show. But at least *Things To Come* offered to a thoughtful few some probing questions about our society's destiny.

Regardless, it took a long time for the picture to recoup its $1.4 million production cost. For its incredible scope and ambitious special effects, however, the film remains a landmark of the science fiction cinema.

The other major contribution of the 30s to the genre was that of the serial. A longtime fixture of the silent films era and of the Western movies, the serial brought science fiction to the mainstream of American movie audiences. Like the Western dime novel, the science fiction pulp magazines' popularity and the resulting success of such comic strips as *Buck Rogers in the 25th Century* and Alex Raymond's *Flash Gordon* helped make them ripe targets for serialization.

Interestingly, a hero of Western serials was probably responsible for hooking millions of kids on Saturday-afternoon science fiction adventure. Singing cowboy Gene Autry starred in 1935's *Phantom Empire* as himself, a

Texas 'rancher' and radio-station operator who discovers a bizarre lost city 20,000 feet under his land. An ensuing scuffle with nasty crooks trying to get at the radium deposited in the land leads our hero and his faithful side-kicks, including Smiley Burnette as Oscar, underground for a series of adventures. The evil Queen Tika of Murania wants her robots (and the ever-present death-ray) to rule the world, but after 13 chapters, Autry and his pals manage to do away with her. No one in the audiences seemed to mind that Autry was wearing six-shooters and fringe throughout.

The best of the serials, though, came in 1936, with Universal's half-million-dollar production of *Flash Gordon*, starring former Olympic swimmer Larry 'Buster' Crabbe and Jean Rogers as his clinging girlfriend Dale Arden. The resounding success of the serial was due in large part to the perfect casting of Crabbe, who not only displayed a convincing devotion to the role over the years, but also bore a striking resemblance to the golden-haired comic strip hero.

Audiences were completely absorbed as Flash led them through 13 weeks of battle against the vicious Ming the Merciless (played with great camp by Charles Middleton). The concept of space flight had until now been completely rejected by the public, but everyone loved to watch Flash and his buddies career effortlessly through space in Dr Zarkov's cardboard contraption.

*Above :* Jean Rogers and Buster Crabbe (with peroxide-blond curls) get an outer-space briefing in Flash Gordon (1936).

*Opposite top :* Buster Crabbe, the former Olympic swimmer, starred in *Flash Gordon* (1936), the first of a series of three serials in which he would appear as the man of the future. Following this there was *Flash Gordon's Trip to Mars* (1938) and *Flash Gordon Conquers the Universe* (1940). Here, after being sentenced to stoke the fires by the evil Ming the Merciless, he leads a revolt, but is subdued. Wait until next week.

*Opposite bottom :* Gene Autry trying to control a robot in another serial, *Phantom Empire* (1935), an incredible story about a cowboy who finds the lost city of Murania four miles below the surface of his Texas land.

33

The serial was followed by two sequels, 1938's *Flash Gordon's Trip to Mars* and *Flash Gordon Conquers the Universe* of 1940, though the overall quality (and budgets) seemed to diminish with each effort. Crabbe even starred in a spin-off of Flash's popularity, the 1939 *Buck Rogers*, whose hero originally appeared as a character in novels by Phillip Frances Nowlan. Each episode contained the same formulation of wild-eyed villain, some sort of threat to mankind (more often than not, the inevitable 'death ray'), a cliff-hanger to sell the following week's episode and an awesome assortment of space-man claptrap: ray guns, anti-gravity belts, clumsy cardboard robots and spaceships, reflectoplate televisors and a zoological parade of menacing ape-men, shark-men, bird-men, fire dragons, octosacs, orangapoids, and (gasp) 'The Gocko'. Science fiction fans were close to heaven.

Unfortunately, Hollywood's producers were so enamored of that success formula that the 1940s produced few interesting or original science fiction pictures. Nearly all of them, as in the 30s, resorted to horror-film tactics to entertain. Any science fiction elements were included only to open up the screen to the realm of the fantastic—and then were unceremoniously dumped.

Perhaps the box-office failure of such intelligent films as *Things To Come* convinced producers that ambitious science fiction topics were best avoided. Something like Wells' remarkable prophetic prediction of world war was, they reasoned, the farthest thing from what the public wanted to see.

Not until 1950 did Hollywood lift itself from the gutter of cheap horror conventions and the mindless entertainment of the serials, with George Pal's *Destination Moon*. Almost a documentary in its approach, this tale of lunar exploration has the distinction of being adapted from a juvenile novel, *Rocketship Galileo*, by one of the masters of science fiction literature, Robert Heinlein. The author himself, as well as rocket expert Hermann Oberth (who had worked 21 years before on Lang's *Die Frau im Mond*) were retained as script consultants, and gave the film a scientific realism unusual to the genre. Director Irving Pichel went to great lengths to recreate the lunar surface as scientists knew it appeared, and to create realistically the effect of weightlessness. Hence, the American public received something of an education on space flight; regrettably, few cared. The story concerns an experimenting scientist who, when his atomic rocket loses government support, seeks the backing of private investors in order to beat the Russians into space. After a successful landing and exploration on the Moon, a fuel shortage is discovered. Happily, discarding all but the bare essentials, the astronauts are able to lift off and return to Earth.

Audiences recognized that for all its special effects and stunning sets and backdrops executed by astronomical artist Chesley Bonestell, *Destination Moon* was boring. That is probably why *Rocketship X-M*, an imitation with a ridiculous but fast-paced plot, did just as well at the box office. Its producer and director, Robert Lippert and Kurt Newmann, heard about Pal's project, and in all of three

*Opposite top :* A scene from *Destination Moon* (1950), a story of an American spaceship that heads for the moon. This was one of the pioneer spaceship science-fiction films, and at the time it was made, the spaceship and its hardware were thought to be remarkably realistic. They may seem a bit on the antique side now, but the other effects, especially those of the moon's surface, remain as impressive as ever.

*Opposite bottom :* Lloyd Bridges (second from left) was the star of *Rocketship X-M*. Here the explorers look around at the deserts of an atomic-destroyed Mars. They were originally going to the moon, but were blown off course. Reaching the market just ahead of *Destination Moon*, this low-budget film earned a lasting place in science-fiction film history because it was the first of the modern pictures to use space travel as a theme.

*Below : Things to Come* (1936) was a film based upon the H G Wells fantasy about the destructive world war that wiped out life as we know it, but which paved the way for a better world. Here people in the world of the future gather before a giant television screen to receive instructions.

weeks shot their 78-minute film—at less than a sixth of *Destination Moon*'s cost—and beat Pal's release.

But both pictures had the effect of inciting Hollywood to pump out a number of cheap imitations and films on other science fiction topics to cash in on the boom the two had started.

Pal followed his success with another science fiction picture called *When Worlds Collide*, directed by Rudolph Mate and released by Paramount in 1951. The Philip Wylie/Edwin Balmer novel of the same name had been acquired in 1934 as a project for Cecil B De Mille—appropriate, because at times the story of Earth's destruction resembles a Bible epic. Interestingly, Pal would later produce another Paramount property De Mille had rejected, *War of the Worlds*.

*When Worlds Collide*, like *Destination Moon*, had no big-name stars. The film tells of a scientist who is convinced that twin planets, Bellus and Zyra, are going to pass through the solar system; Zyra will fall into the Earth's orbit around the Sun, and Bellus will strike our planet days later, obliterating both worlds. A billionaire agrees to fund a hasty escape rocket to be launched at Zyra, providing he can be guaranteed a seat. The remainder of the film is similar to any of Hollywood's lifeboat movies; who will be chosen to survive? Of course, various love interests and cowardly attempts to foil the selection process crop up, but in the end, the rocket zooms off its curved runway. During flight, the ship almost runs out of fuel, but somehow safely deposits the survivors of Earth's destruction on Zyra's picture-postcard surface.

The film's most impressive moments deal with the Earth's natural disasters, including the flooding of New York City, and ultimate doom as the result of the planets' collision. Much credit for the effects goes to Paramount's Oscar-winning head of special effects, Gordon Jennings, who teamed with Pal on other science fiction films.

*When Worlds Collide* featured a popular fifties theme—total annihilation, which probably reflected the public's fear of an atomic catastrophe. Another 1951 film, released by RKO, *The Thing*, touched off an even bigger gold rush in Hollywood, alien invasion on the big screen.

Very loosely taken from John W Campbell's short novel, *Who Goes There!* Christian Nyby's tidy film, also called *The Thing From Another World*, took full advantage of the UFO craze America was experiencing at the time, and though it is low on actual scientific content, it is the forerunner of, in fact it is *the* archetypal paranoia movie.

The simple plot concerns the discovery of an alien and its spaceship frozen into the Arctic wastelands near an Army outpost. Having thawed out, a giant living plant creature, resembling an oversize carrot, begins a murder binge to collect the human blood it needs to feed its young. Produced by Hollywood's famous Howard Hawks, the picture is fast-paced and entertaining, but the ending sadly reflected audiences' attitudes toward scientists at the time. The well-meaning researchers want to study the creature, but, with a dose of good old Yankee common

sense, an Army captain has the creature blown away before things really get out of hand.

Another alien receives a similar reception in 1951's Fox release of *The Day the Earth Stood Still*, directed by Robert Wise. Michael Rennie sensitively portrays Klaatu, a visitor whose mission is to put an end to the petty hostilities of the Earthlings before they wipe themselves out. Klaatu meets with much resistance, but after an interlude with a friendly woman played by Patricia Neal, he and his robot manage to get their message across to a group of government bureaucrats and military officials: grow up and lay down your arms, or we'll be forced to exterminate you.

The film's intelligent script and a top-notch cast help make *The Day The Earth Stood Still* a better-than-average flying saucer epic, but like other standout films of the 50s, it did little to encourage more of the same quality.

The year 1953, though, was an excellent year for science fiction, and saw George Pal's treatment of the H G Wells classic, *War of the Worlds*. Pal changed the setting of Wells' tale of Martian invasion from the English countryside to Southern California, and updated the time frame to the 1950s. Gene Barry and Ann Robinson starred as a nuclear physicist and his girl on the run. An enemy force of flying machines, complete with disintegrating heat rays, are smashing up the Earth in a spectacular campaign of destruction. Just when the end looms near, our heroes huddling in a church in demolished Los Angeles, the Martian machines collapse. Their pilots have succumbed to tiny, ordinary bacteria which they had not anticipated, and to which they have no immunity.

Byron Haskin's efficient direction, and some of the most gripping moments of science fiction destruction, help compensate for Pal's usual weak plotting and characterization. Paramount's crack special effects team was the film's real star, and won Pal's third Oscar for a science fiction movie.

By 1953, most of the major themes of the science fiction cinema had been developed, save the idea of alien possession, the horrifying use of other humans to further unworldly motives. The picture that started the ball rolling,

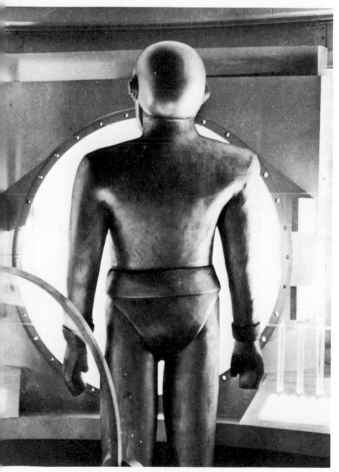

*Top :* Some of the passengers brace for the blastoff in *When Worlds Collide* (1951). The special effects, for the time, were considered to be outstanding. It told the story of the discovery that a runaway planetoid would crash into the earth and destroy it, and the feverish activity in building a rocket ship that would take an elite contingent safely away just before the collision.

*Left :* One of the most thoughtful science-fiction films was *The Day the Earth Stood Still* (1951), which brought the alien Klaatu (Michael Rennie) to Earth for the purpose of warning that future excesses in nuclear power and space work would result in self-annihilation. Here, Patricia Neal confronts Klaatu's faithful robot companion.

*It Came From Outer Space*, was also the first science fiction 3-D film of the fifties. Directed by Jack Arnold of Universal Studios, the film is remarkably quiet and thoughtful, considering its theme.

Richard Carlson appeared as a witness to the emergency landing of a huge UFO. He tries to tell the inhabitants of a small, nearby Arizona town of what he has seen, but he is ignored until various citizens of the town begin to act strangely; the aliens are using them to obtain the materials they need to repair their spacecraft so that they can escape. Finally sensing trouble, the villagers attempt to disable the vehicle, but the blob-like creatures release the humans and blast off in the nick of time.

*It Came from Outer Space* was liberally adapted from a Ray Bradbury tale, though the first movie to claim that distinction was *The Beast from 20,000 Fathoms*. Somehow, Bradbury's fascinating tale of a dinosaur seeking its mate after hearing an ordinary foghorn was muddled in a B-grade horror flick. But the film did spark an almost unending prehistoric-monster film binge. These almost always, as in *The Beast*, supposed that atomic radiation had somehow brought back to life various antagonists. At least such monsters weren't as threatening to audiences as the bomb itself, which they were meant to symbolize.

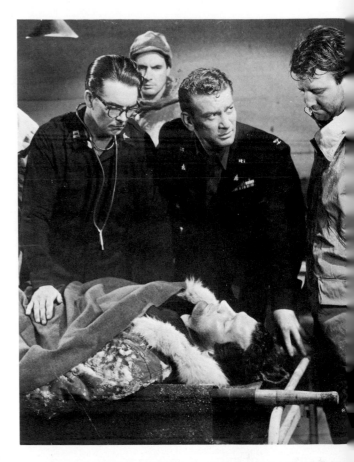

The concept of atomic power wasn't new to science fiction. In fact, Jules Verne wrote of an atomic-powered submarine in his 1870 *20,000 Leagues Under the Sea*. Walt Disney's version of the Verne classic, the fourth such adaptation, was a standout because of the 'period' treatment—the vessel *Nautilus* looks as fantastic and Gothic as Verne himself might have imagined it to be. The 1954 film, directed by Richard Fleischer, featured an impressive cast including Kirk Douglas, Peter Lorre and James Mason in the best interpretation of the Captain Nemo role ever put on film. Much of the production's $5 million budget went toward the impressive underwater special effects, especially the giant squid battle scene. The film remains a classic, despite the script's occasional sentimentalization, and is re-released regularly.

Improving the genre's lot was left to the 1956 MGM big-budget epic *Forbidden Planet*, directed by Fred McLeod Wilcox. Loosely based on Shakespeare's *The Tempest*, the story concerns a space patrol mission in search of a lost expeditionary force on the planet Altair IV. Upon arrival, several of the crew are attacked by a mysterious invisible monster. The colony's only survivors, Dr Morbius (Walter Pidgeon) and his daughter (Anne Francis) are unable to explain anything. Commander Adams (Leslie Nielsen) soon gets to the bottom of things, however, and learns of the Krell, an extinct race of superbeings who have left behind machinery capable of turning thought into matter. The victims were literally killed by the monsters of their own bestial subconscious thoughts.

Adams finds that the monster causing all the trouble is that of Morbius' own mind. Only after more death and destruction is Morbius convinced of this, and he suppresses the creature long enough for the others to escape the

planet. As Adams and the daughter do so, Morbius destroys Altair IV.

*Forbidden Planet* was the first science fiction movie to feature a military space organization, to which *Star Trek* of television owes so much. It also featured the first in a long line of personable robots, the famous Robby. The film is also noted for its pioneering electronic musical score, and some superior special effects, including the Disney-animated monster.

In choosing the best science fiction film of the eventful 50s, many argue between *Forbidden Planet* and another classic, *Invasion of the Body Snatchers*, perhaps one of the most terrifying alien possession pictures ever. Skillfully directed by Don Siegel, the 1956 Allied Artists picture starred Kevin McCarthy as Miles Bennell, who returns to his home town of Santa Mira, California from a vacation. He discovers that many of the townspeople have turned eerily passive. He and his former girlfriend Becky (Dana Wynter) visit a friend whose greenhouse contains a giant pod that slowly begins to resemble that friend—and finally comes to life.

*Above :* In *It Came from Outer Space* (1953), ectoplasmic forces from the space world materialize in a doorway and eerily confront scientist John Putnam (Richard Carlson).

*Opposite top :* A victim of *The Beast from 20,000 Fathoms* (1953) is examined. The picture told the story (on a low budget) of a rampaging giant lizard. It had good special effects and the distinction of having a screenplay written by Ray Bradbury, the renowned science-fiction author.

*Opposite bottom :* In a late 1970s remake of *The Invasion of the Body Snatchers*, health inspector Dr Matthew Bennell (Donald Sutherland) discovers some strange growth in a friend's garden. One of the gimmicks in this remake was having Kevin McCarthy, the star of the first version, in a walk-on part.

Realizing that the pods are taking over the entire population and murdering the original bodies, Miles and Becky attempt to flee, but are hunted down by the entire village, now transformed. Becky succumbs, but Miles somehow escapes and is found wandering down a freeway near Los Angeles. Picked up by police and hospitalized, he tells his gruesome tale to an unbelieving group; only when a truckful of pods is discovered does his doctor call in the FBI. The film ends on the optimistic note that we may be saved.

*Invasion of the Body Snatchers* was so popular as a cult film in later years that it spawned a remake in 1978, starring Donald Sutherland and Margot Kidder in the lead roles, with a chilling performance by Leonard Nimoy (television's Mr Spock) as a psychiatrist and alien accomplice. The original film's ambivalent treatment of the idea of conformity has been called both McCarthyite and anti-fascist—in any event it is a fascinating parable of survival in an environment where even friends cannot be trusted.

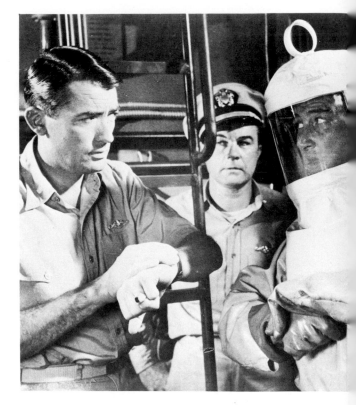

Few dramatic performances in science fiction films have surpassed that of Grant Williams as Scott Carey, *The Incredible Shrinking Man*. Universal's expert science fiction and horror director, Jack Arnold, neatly wove this 1957 tale of a man who mysteriously begins to reduce in size in an irreversible pattern. As he continues to shrink, confounding scientists and doctors, Carey must learn to survive at a previously ignored, small-scale level. Here, things like the family cat, staircases, and ultimately, household spiders, become major obstacles. What is unique in the film is the subsequent growth in the maturity and values of Carey as an adult. By the time he is small enough to wander through a screen window and into the garden, he has convinced himself that there must be some purpose to it all. These are not fatuous notions; rather, they are the courageous and serene words of a man totally at grips with his destiny.

Particularly memorable in *The Incredible Shrinking Man*

are the use of props and ingenious matté effects to depict Carey's changing size in proportion to his environment, and sparse, unsentimental writing. The film was adapted by Richard Matheson from his original novel of the same title.

Closing out the 50s was an outstanding film not recognized by the public as science fiction (hence, perhaps, its widespread acceptance)—1959's *On the Beach*, based on the novel by Nevil Shute. Regardless, Shute's drama of the last days of some Southern Hemisphere survivors of an atomic holocaust is distinctly science fiction. Gregory Peck stars as the captain of an American submarine detailed to Australia; Ava Gardner and Fred Astaire play Australians who, along with their countrymen, desperately try to find a dignified or glorious way to die. Producer and director Stanley Kramer gave the United Artists film a sober tone, and it remains today an effective statement about man's aggressive, and ultimately suicidal, tendencies.

Such films as *On the Beach* and others released during the early 60s marked the entry of the science fiction film into the mainstream of American cinema. Previously regarded as a genre for smaller film companies and hack production outfits, science fiction began to draw attention from big-studio producers and directors as a viable means of addressing the new decade's more complex issues.

Even the thriller was becoming more sophisticated, the B-grade movies having all but burned themselves out. An example of this increased sophistication was *Village of the Damned*, a British film released by MGM in the United

*Above :* A sequel to *Village of the Damned* (1960) was *Children of the Damned* (1964). Those children with the strange luminous eyes were even more menacing in this one. They really feel their strange powers, setting their target as the destruction of the whole world. Unfortunately, it was not as imaginative as the original.

*Opposite top :* In *On the Beach* (1959) Gregory Peck (left), as the submarine commander, prepares a crew member for the exploration of a radiation-poisoned city. The film was adapted from the Nevil Shute novel and set in Australia. It is the story of a group of people (including the officers and crew of an American submarine) awaiting death from a radioactive cloud that, in the wake of a nuclear holocaust, has destroyed all life in the Northern Hemisphere and is now spreading over the rest of the world.

*Opposite bottom :* *Village of the Damned* (1960) starred George Sanders and Barbara Shelley (far left) plus a group of big-eyed, all-powerful kids bent on destruction of everyone and everything. It was an outstanding low-budget shocker.

States in 1960. Based on John Wyndham's *The Midwich Cuckoos*, Wolf Rilla's low-key film tells the story of a small English village which is taken by a bizzare alien attack: all the town's women of child-bearing age are made pregnant. The resulting generation has the gift of telepathic communication and a manipulative power of suggestion over the citizenry. One man sees that they are bound to take over the world, and in some highly suspenseful scenes manages to destroy the children.

The cool, emotionless appearance of the children is extremely affecting, and *Village of the Damned* not only prompted a sequel, 1963's *Children of the Damned*, but pointed the way for future 'possessed children' movies.

In the same year, George Pal directed a second H G Wells adaptation, with Rod Taylor in the lead role of MGM's *The Time Machine*. Like many films based on works by Wells and Verne, *The Time Machine* was filmed as a period piece, with an appropriately ornate device and its matching special effects stealing the show. Another interesting period film of the following year, 1961, featured Vincent Price and Charles Bronson in a Verne borrowing. William Witney's *Master of the World* faithfully follows Verne's tale of a scientist and the crew of his fantastic 19th century airship and their attempts to stop human aggression by destroying war vessels at sea. Price gives an appropriate blend of both fiend and humanitarian in the Nemo-like role of Robur the Conqueror. Bronson plays his foil, a government agent who sets out to destroy Robur's craft, the *Albatross*.

A far more stunning message about mankind's bent for self-destruction can be found in *Dr Strangelove; or, How I Learned to Stop Worrying and Love the Bomb*, a 1963

*Opposite top : The Time Machine* (1963) was based upon H G Wells' novel of the same name. Rod Taylor travels far into the future to a place where humanlike people, the Eloi, are the slaves of hairy monsters, the Morlocks. Here Taylor, as the time traveler, fights the wicked Morlocks as the terrified Eloi look on.

*Opposite bottom :* In one of his three different character portrayals—that in the title role in *Dr Strangelove or How I Learned to Stop Worrying and Love the Bomb*—Peter Sellers enters the room in his wheelchair. The film was the first nuclear comedy, full of black humor about the destruction of the entire earth.

*Below :* A frightened Rod Taylor in his Time Machine.

*Bottom :* Part of the crew of the airship in *Master of the World* (1961).

Columbia film. The first of Stanley Kubrick's three great science fiction films, *Dr Strangelove* is black comedy and science fiction both. Peter Sellers captures the audience with performances in three roles, including Dr Strangelove, the hapless President Muffley and a Royal Air Force officer, Lionel Mandrake. Sterling Hayden plays General Jack D Ripper who orders a squadron of B-52s to unload all of their atomic bombs on Russia. Under the impression that a war is declared, the pilots ignore the pleas of the military and even President Muffley for a retreat, thinking this is only a Russian trick. Finally, the military storms Ripper's sealed-off air base and obtains his secret recall codes, despite his suicide. All of the jets retreat, except that of Major T J 'King' Kong (Slim Pickens), whose radio has been knocked out. Like a cowboy on a loco horse, Kong rides his prize nuclear warhead all the way down, and World War III is started. Our last vision is of giant mushroom clouds, and we hear Vera Lynn singing, 'We'll Meet Again'.

Kubrick's message was searingly anti-establishment for its time, especially in its portrayal of an almost psychotic military, with brilliant comic performances by Hayden, Keenan Wynn and George C Scott. *Dr Strangelove* has been called everything from one of the finest films ever made, to the worst of sick jokes. Such widely varying criticism is not unusual for any Kubrick film, but most agree that *Dr Strangelove* is the best film on nuclear war to date.

Another major event for the science fiction cinema of the 60s was the 1962 appearance of Sean Connery as Agent 007 in *Dr No*. Though it and subsequent James Bond films are regarded mostly as spy adventures, each plot typically progresses into a science fiction world right out of *Flash Gordon*. Here we find vast underground or undersea complexes created by mad scientists bent on world domination, who by coincidence are often either German or Oriental in descent—or both!

The 007 films through the years have become increasingly 'sci-fi', perhaps culminating with 1979's *Moonraker*. Particularly memorable is 1967's *You Only Live Twice* which featured a lavish underground rocket base, the set for which was built on the back lot of Pinewood Studios in England at the expense of half a million dollars.

The mid-60s were not great years for science fiction films. Probably the best rendition ever of a Ray Bradbury novel was created by Francois Truffaut, though, in 1966's *Fahrenheit 451*, released by Universal Studios. The story's main character, Montag (Oskar Werner), is a fireman who *starts* book fires—his future-world's government has banned the ownership or reading of books. Montag's wife, played by Julie Christie, like the rest of society, stays glued to her wall television, controlled by the government. One day, during a routine book burning, Montag witnesses an old woman's suicide. She has chosen to die rather than part with her books. Moved by this, Montag joins an underground community of 'living books'—each member

*Opposite top :* In *You Only Live Twice* (1967), Sean Connery as James Bond flies a spy mission in one of the strange vehicles that have been designed over the years for the 007 films. This was the fifth of the Bond pictures.

*Opposite bottom :* *Fahrenheit 451* (1966) was named after the temperature at which books will burn. Here the secret police are on a raid to collect the outlawed reading matter. Written by Ray Bradbury, the film tells of how a rebel segment of the people dedicates itself to get around the campaign of burning all the world's great literature by memorizing all the books that are available or that they can remember.

*Below :* An enormous set for another James Bond movie— *Moonraker* (1979). The Russian rocket on its pad.

has completely memorized one book to preserve it, and hence becomes that book.

Bradbury's effective poetic message on the value of free expression loses something in Truffaut's intentionally quiet and uninvolved film. It is mostly the romantic metaphor of 'living books' that is difficult to translate on film. But *Fahrenheit 451* retains its most important values and remains a significant film to remember.

The same year, 1966, brought high-budget special effects in the Richard Fleischer film, *Fantastic Voyage*. A completely ridiculous tale of a submarine task force miniaturized in order to enter the bloodstream of a scientist and try to remove an inoperable blood clot, *Fantastic Voyage* was a huge success. That success was due in large part to its innovative special effects and a variety of sets depicting arteries and organs as colorful as a Peter Max poster. Raquel Welch, Arthur Kennedy, Stephen Boyd and Donald Pleasance all portrayed rather shallow and uninteresting characters, at least not upstaging the artistry of the sets.

Even more successful was 1968's *Planet of the Apes*, directed by Franklin J Schaffner and starring the award-winning makeup of John Chambers more than anything else. Charlton Heston and Roddy McDowall co-starred in the tale of four American astronauts who are accidentally sent to a world where apes reign and where humans are speechless idiots. The captive astronauts are either

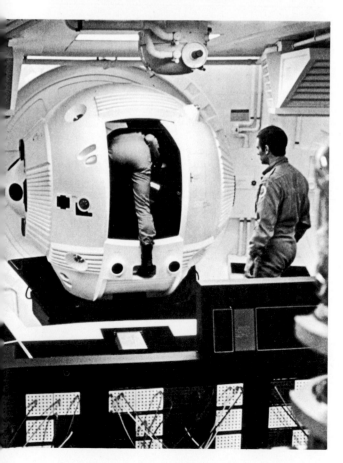

killed or experimented with, but, befriended by two scientist apes, spaceman Heston escapes the ape city. He forages north to the Forbidden Lands where, lo and behold, he discovers the half-buried Statue of Liberty on an abandoned beach—he has somehow been trapped in the Earth's future.

The convincing makeup by Chambers and the fantastic plot line propelled *The Planet of the Apes* into a series with no less than four sequels, extrapolated from the original novel by Pierre Boulle: *Beneath the Planet of the Apes, Escape from the Planet of the Apes, Conquest of the Planet of the Apes* and *Battle for the Planet of the Apes,* released from 1970 to 1973. Though the long-running epic became more improbable with each episode, it was a huge financial success, leading to two television series and many book adaptations.

But a far more lasting success story began in 1968, with MGM's release of Stanley Kubrick's *2001 : A Space Odyssey.* That story owes to the collaboration of director Kubrick and distinguished science fiction author Arthur C Clarke, and his original short story entitled *The Sentinel.*

Some call *2001* three different movies. Indeed, the film is divided into three parts with separate time frames and characters. The only tangible link, much to the confusion of audiences and critics, is a massive black monolith.

The parable begins with a prehistoric prologue in which we witness that momentuous turning point in human evolution, the point at which our ancestral relatives, the apes, became users of tools. By no accident, Kubrick has paralleled the first use of tools with the first use of weapons. This realistic scene departs from science in its suggestion that the turning point has been caused by intervention from an alien force, represented by the monolith.

We then are brought to the year 2001, where once again, the monolith, discovered under the powdery soil of American Moon territory, is exerting its influence on humans. Dr Heywood Floyd and his fellow scientists gather at the excavation site to examine the monolith, and are nearly overcome by a powerful radio signal. Its target: the moons of Jupiter.

In the final episode of the trilogy, an expedition to find out what lies at the other end of the signal is underway. Astronauts Poole, Bowman and several others in suspended animation are joined by HAL-9000, a soft-spoken computer, in a giant spacecraft appropriately named 'Discovery.' Problems arise when HAL, super-intelligent but inbred with human weakness, starts going mad. Burdened with the mission's secret, he becomes convinced that the astronauts want to de-program him, and succeeds in killing all but Bowman. The lone survivor, however, manages to turn HAL off.

Bowman then proceeds in one of the Discovery's space pods toward one of Jupiter's moons, where he encounters the black monolith. It propels him through a spectacular light show, presumably a voyage to another time or dimension. His final encounter with the monolith causes him rapidly to age and die; then he experiences a rebirth.

*Above :* Astronaut Lloyd (Gene Hackman) sits in the cockpit of his spaceship patiently awaiting a rescue ship from Earth while marooned in space—from *Marooned* (1969).

*Opposite top :* Cliff Robertson and Claire Bloom starred in *Charly* (1968). Robertson won the Academy Award for his portrayal of a mentally retarded bakery worker whose IQ is drastically raised through surgery. He becomes a super-brain, but his brilliant mind lets him calculate that it is a temporary thing and he will lose his intelligence. Bloom played his sympathetic social worker.

*Opposite bottom :* In *Marooned* (1969), the rescue ship approaches the three trapped astronauts. The special effects in this movie won an Academy Award.

The transformation is complete, and the embryo of Starchild Bowman floats toward Earth.

Despite its flaws in plot, *2001* has proven itself immensely popular over the years, and much of its entertainment value lies in the discussion of its meaning. No two people are likely to agree about it, and Clarke and Kubrick are of no help—the film has been intentionally stripped of any meaningful characters or dialogue, a possible exception being HAL's role. Yet Kubrick has gone so far as to allow that the film may be a sort of blend of theology and science. Aliens, he has said, might easily be seen by humans as gods. Is the black monolith a scientific likeness of God?

Kubrick told *Playboy* in 1968, 'I don't want to spell out a verbal road map of *2001* that every viewer will feel obligated to pursue or else fear he's missed the point.' While he certainly succeeded to that end, the film remains to many boring, ambiguous, and disjointed at times. Some suggest that all this reflects the qualities of man's prolonged development. It is nonetheless memorable cinema.

Perhaps most memorable are the special effects. Kubrick spent six years and more than $10 million seeing to it that every detail of the picture is totally believable, and he succeeded. Stars William Sylvester, Keir Dullea and Gary Lockwood played a distinct second fiddle to the painstakingly composed and executed special effects. Each element dealing with space travel is completely convincing —at no moment does the viewer feel that he is watching a contrivance of models and optical processes. Two-thirds of the film's budget was spent on the special effects. A team of Wally Veevers, Tom Howard, Con Pederson and Douglas Trumbull ensured their effectiveness.

*2001* not only redefined the use and technical methods of special effects, but at last made science fiction fully respectable in the eyes of major producers. MGM's huge investment paid off slowly but handsomely, and other producers were encouraged to take the genre seriously and pay closer heed to the long-ignored ideas of science fiction writers.

A different type of science fiction film, indeed serious, was 1968's *Charly*. Its star, Cliff Robertson, won an Oscar for his portrayal of a retarded adult whose intelligence is significantly raised through medical experimentation. Robertson is excellent at showing how a man might feel if suddenly experiencing the emotions of love and sexuality for the first time, and of becoming a genius. The operation turns out to be only temporary, and before long, Charly is experiencing a horrible regression, realizing that any hopes for a normal life have been dashed. The film, though awkward at times, retains much of the sentiment of Daniel Keyes' novel, *Flowers for Algernon*, on which it is based.

Closing out the 60s was the 1969 Columbia production of *Marooned*, directed by John Sturges. It starred Gregory Peck, David Janssen, Gene Hackman and James Franciscus in a tale of an American space mission that can't get back to Earth because of rocket failure. The ensuing tragedies and rescue form a silly, sentimental plot, but the picture won that year's Oscar for special effects, which paled in comparison to those of *2001*.

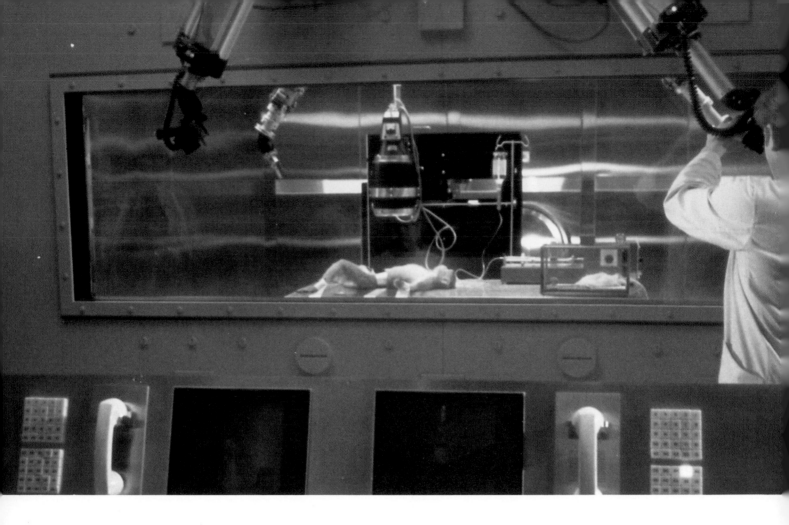

*Above :* One of the survivors of the deadly virus that has been brought back to the Earth by a space probe being tested in the quarantined laboratory in *The Andromeda Strain* (1971).

*Opposite top :* A scene from *A Clockwork Orange* (1971). The film was a shattering political allegory about a loathsome, violent anti-hero in a modern society where young punks run amok and peaceful citizens are imprisoned in their own homes. It was based upon a novel by Anthony Burgess which was partially autobiographical, as Burgess' own wife was robbed, raped and severely beaten by three GI deserters during a World War II blackout in London. She later died of her injuries.

*Opposite center :* Malcolm McDowell in *A Clockwork Orange*. He was altogether chilling playing a pathological toughie. After the initial release, Stanley Kubrick, who was the producer, writer and director, re-edited *Clockwork* slightly to make it less violent.

*Opposite bottom :* A victim of violence in *Slaughterhouse-Five* (1972), based upon the novel by Kurt Vonnegut.

While the 1970s did not see a record number of science fiction films, the genre had matured to the point where more sophisticated stories and improvements in both effects and cinematography allowed a number of intelligent, creative entries.

Among them was 1971's *Andromeda Strain*, another Robert Wise film, released by Universal. The story, written by Michael Crichton, a doctor turned writer and director, was faithfully followed by screenwriter Nelson Giddings. It tells of a deadly virus accidentally carried from space to Earth by a returning space probe. After wiping out all but two inhabitants of a small town, the virus, as well as the two survivors and a team of scientists, is isolated in a special germ-control laboratory to find out how to combat the microorganism. By the time the scientists learn of the virus' nature and avoid near disaster, the organism has mutated into forms harmless to man.

*The Andromeda Strain*'s ending is somewhat anti-climactic for audiences, but James Olson, Arthur Hill, David Wayne and Kate Reid deliver controlled performances as scientists who have become dominated by technology itself, in this case, the laboratory's controlling computer. The settings are stark and antiseptic-looking, and the electronic gadgetry is worth the great expense. Special effects absorbed much of the film's $6.5 million budget.

Another important science fiction film of 1971, *A Clockwork Orange*, was director Stanley Kubrick's third

foray into the genre. Based on Anthony Burgess' novel, the film is a highly pessimistic message about our culture which both breeds and barbarically suppresses violence. The conditioning of an incorrigible gangster to abhor violence, with techniques that are equally inhuman, backfires. Malcolm McDowell delivers a chilling performance as the criminal savage who, despite his utter lack of morality, deserves pity as the victim of a ruthless, immoral government and its self-centered manipulation of the people.

*A Clockwork Orange* became completely embroiled in controversy upon release due to its graphic scenes of violence, and had to be diluted somewhat before it was acceptable to widespread audiences. But its shattering theme remains intact, and the film is regarded by many as Kubrick's finest.

Fledgling filmmaker George Lucas got his start in 1971 with the theatrical release of *THX 1138*, based on a short work he produced as a student at the University of Southern California. Concerning a future state that controls the lives of its underground inhabitants, the film stars Robert Duvall as a worker whose daily drug dose is inadvertently diminished. Faced with stark reality, THX 1138 becomes a fugitive on the run. Only after the state determines that they are over budget in chasing him do they allow him to escape to the surface.

The following year brought the film version of Kurt Vonnegut's novel *Slaughterhouse-Five*, directed by George Roy Hill and produced by Universal. It is the story of a middle-aged American who suddenly begins to drift into his past and future lives: his past, scenes from his imprisonment in Germany during World War II; his future, life after death as a prisoner on the planet Trafalmador, where he is kept in a cage with a sexpot (Valerie Perrine) as a zoo attraction. Michael Sachs portrays Billy Pilgrim, who has become 'unstuck' in time and has given up trying to make sense of things in a totally senseless universe. Some of Vonnegut's dark humor is lost in the novel's film translation, but *Slaughterhouse-Five* retains its effective irony.

Charlton Heston went from starring in Bible epics in his early career to appearing in science fiction and disaster films, such as *Planet of the Apes* and *The Omega Man*, later on. In the latter, a 1971 film directed by Boris Sagal, he portrayed the sole survivor of a plague that has transformed the rest of the world's population into violent, germ-ridden albino creatures. Heston's character, a scientist who accidentally helped to create the disease, must wage an almost helpless one-man war against the creatures.

In 1973, Heston fought another of his typical one-man battles in a straight science fiction film, *Soylent Green*, based on Harry Harrison's novel *Make Room! Make Room!* Heston and producer Walter Seltzer were long interested in the story of a future police detective trying to cope in the corrupt and half-starved society of New York City, 1999. Only when the two added the shocker premise that the state is recycling human bodies to feed the population did MGM agree to support the venture. The result is an interesting, well-acted film (including Edward G Robinson's final screen performance) of survival in the future, marred only by a hokey ending. Our hero, detective Heston, having discovered the terrible secret, is gunned down and carried off screaming 'Soylent Green is people!' The hope is that someone is listening, or even cares.

Intentionally funny, however, was 1973's *Sleeper*, Woody Allen's science fiction farce about a modern-day Rip Van Winkle, awakened after a 200-year deep-freeze sleep by scientists in the year 2173. Allen manages to send up *Brave New World, 1984*, and just about every other piece of science fiction ever written. Best of all, it is hilarious, a good dose of parody in a period when science fiction filmmakers took themselves so seriously. *Sleeper*'s cast included Allen himself and a young Diane Keaton, involved in a complicated plot as absurd as any of the comedian's early works.

Another film based on material by Michael Crichton came in 1973, and this time was even directed by the same. MGM's *Westworld* starred Richard Benjamin, James Brolin and Yul Brynner in a story about a futuristic amusement park where fantasy environments are created for wealthy customers. For $1000 per day, a vacationer can enjoy women, wine and song, and even mow down menacing robot bad-guys, in Medievalworld, Romanworld or Westworld.

The plot thickens when two tourists enjoying Westworld find that the robots have gone out of control, knocking out the control center. One of them, among other tourists, is

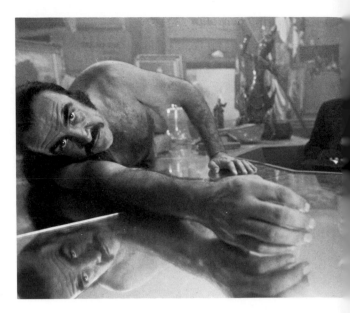

*Top*: Sean Connery in *Zardoz* (1974). Connery played an exterminator hired to keep the lower classes under control.

*Above*: Woody Allen, as a 20th-century man propelled 200 years into the future in *Sleeper* (1973), masquerading as a robot-servant. Little does he know that his head may be switched to another robot.

*Top*: Woody Allen and Diane Keaton try to escape their pursuers in *Sleeper* (1973), a film set in the 22nd century.

*Above*: *Future World* (1976) was a sequel to *Westworld* (1973), and also involved a revolt of the robots. Here Peter Fonda (center) and Stuart Margolin contemplate the problem.

gunned down, and the remainder of the picture is a suspenseful cat-and-mouse adventure between the surviving tourist (Benjamin) and an automated gunfighter (Brynner).

The film was a smash box-office success, and a sequel, *Futureworld*, starring Peter Fonda and Blythe Danner, was released by American International in 1976. But that film, directed by Richard T Heffron, is somewhat implausible for the same reason *Westworld* was—audiences ask, why did the robots revolt in the first place? In the sequel, the robots go so far as to program themselves into a plan for world domination, and the problem of incredibility persists.

The year 1974 was marked by two interesting, if not vastly successful, science fiction films, including the Fox release of *Zardoz*, written, directed and produced by John Boorman. Sean Connery starred in this epic of Earth in the year 2293 which, after atomic catastrophe, has evolved into a world divided between the intelligent, elite Eternals, and the Brutals, whose population is controlled by Connery's group of Exterminators.

The film becomes a presumptuous diatribe on life and death when Zed, one of the Exterminators, finds his way into the protected world of the Eternals and shows them a thing or two about the humanity they have forgotten: sex, violence, love and hate. Society for the Eternals has become a stalemate where even death would be an enjoyable experience. When the hero brings the city's protective force field down, the attacking Exterminators give them just that. Zed takes a wife, of course, and lives out his life as nature meant life to be.

The other film is a rousing satire, filmed as a student project by John Carpenter and Dan O'Bannon, *Dark Star*. The film turns the premise of *Star Trek* around: a space-happy crew is sent into the galaxies to wipe out 'unstable' planets, not to explore or help them. The shoestring-budgeted picture was later made into a theatrical release, and is occasionally seen on late-night television re-runs. No science fiction fan should miss it.

*Top*: Lord Darth Vader, the villain of *Star Wars* (1977), *The Empire Strikes Back* (1980) and *Return of the Jedi* (1983), played by David Prowse but with the voice of James Earl Jones.

*Above*: The fierce but lovable Wookie, Chewbacca.

*Opposite top*: A moment of action from *Rollerball* (1975).

*Opposite bottom*: Michael York and Jenny Agutter are captured in *Logan's Run* (1976).

Of striking contrast is Norman Jewison's science fiction thriller, *Rollerball*, released by United Artists in 1975. James Caan portrayed a superstar in the sport of Rollerball, a violent cross between hockey and roller derby, which has been created by the world-ruling corporations to satisfy the masses. Jonathan E (Caan) is too good a player; after 10 successful years, the corporations fear that he is becoming a disturbing symbol of permanence in a world where individuality is to be downplayed. Thus, they change the game to become increasingly violent in order to exterminate him. But to the dismay of the top executives, Jonathan somehow wipes out all of his competitors. The deafening cheers of the public, signaling a triumph of man over conformity, mark Jonathan E's final game.

*Rollerball* is a slow film, except for its graphically violent sports scenes, meant to tell audiences something about the nature of spectator games. An even slower-paced picture, *Logan's Run*, was released by MGM in 1976. Adapted from William F Nolan and George Clayton Johnson's novel, the film was directed by Michael Anderson. Michael York portrays Logan-5, a 'Sandman' who helps to kill citizens on their 30th birthdays in order to control the population in a domed, computer-run city of the year 2274. When he is assigned to find out where some resisters are escaping to, he learns the true nature of mankind; in the desolate outside world, it is possible to age beyond 30, and live with one woman and family until death by natural causes. When Logan and his heroine, played by Jenny Agutter, try to tell the citizens of their discovery, there is a riot. The city is destroyed and its inhabitants will be forced to live out their lives the way nature meant life to be.

If that seems to be a redundant theme of the 70s—technology isn't as good for us as the basic nature of man, or God's will—then the fan will be refreshed by George Lucas' 1977 *Star Wars*, released by Fox. Though both *Logan's Run* and this film are heavy on special effects, and good ones at that, *Star Wars* never pretends to lay down a message. It is escapist entertainment in its purest form.

That is exactly what George Lucas wanted to create, a modern treatment of the *Flash Gordon* genre of pulp science fiction. In fact, he tried to obtain the rights to *Flash Gordon*, but unable to do so, he wrote his own fantasy, using elements from Edgar Rice Burroughs novels, comic strips, old war movies, and more.

The comic-strip plot concerns the adventures of Luke Skywalker (Mark Hamill) who leaves the drab confines of his uncle's farm on the desert planet of Tatooine to join the search for a kidnapped princess. Skywalker enlists the aid of the last of the Jedi Knights, an order of one-time guardians of justice who use a mystical 'force' of good over evil, the old Ben Kenobi (Alec Guinness). Joined by a rough-neck mercenary spaceship captain, Han Solo (Harrison Ford) and his alien Wookie co-pilot Chewbacca and a pair of 'cute' robots, C-3PO and R2-D2, the heroes are off to the Death Star, headquarters of the evil Empire.

There, Princess Leia Organa (Carrie Fisher) is being held by the decadent Grand Moff Tarkin and his black-hooded evildoer, Darth Vader, Dark Lord of the Sith. After innumerable battles and impressive dogfights in space, fought with a blend of cunning and blind faith in 'the force,' Luke and his pals rescue the princess, and the Dark Star is destroyed. Conveniently, Vadar escapes so that he might live to see the sequels.

Creator George Lucas concedes that the plot is intentionally unbelievable and the dialogue simple-minded, neatly dismissing most of the criticism against *Star Wars*. We are left with a picture that is lots of fun to watch, and which, Lucas hopes, will enrich the world of fantasy for today's generation of youngsters, just as he was enriched by the science fiction genre when he was a boy.

The film's visual aspects are often compared, for some strange reason, with those of Kubrick's *2001 : A Space*

*Opposite top :* Luke Skywalker faces the enemy in *Star Wars*.

*Opposite bottom :* Lord Darth Vader (right) and Ben (Obi-Wan) Kenobi (David Prowse and Alec Guinness) battle with light sabers on the *Imperial Death Star* in *Star Wars*.

*Below :* The banquet aboard Darth Vader's ship in *The Empire Strikes Back* (1980). Back row, left to right, Lando Carlrissian (Billy Dee Williams) and Chewbacca. Front row, Princess Leia Organa (Carrie Fisher) and Han Solo (Harrison Ford).

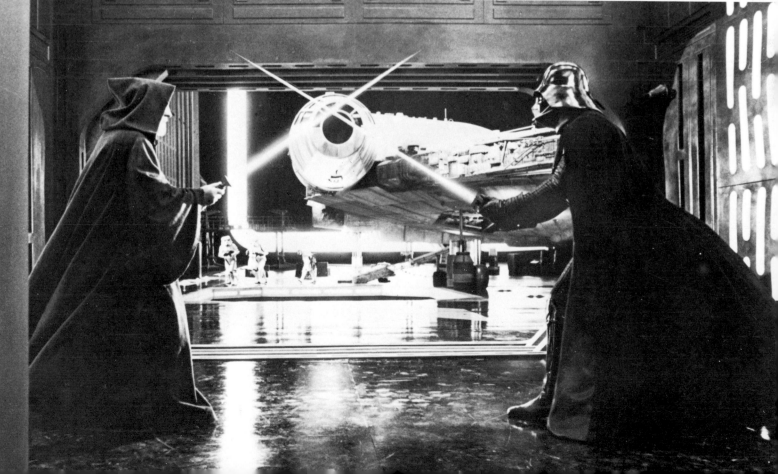

*Odyssey.* The latter is a masterpiece of special effects designed to reflect scientific authenticity, whereas Lucas himself admitted to *Rolling Stone* in 1977 that he 'just wanted to forget science . . . Once the atomic bomb came everybody got into monsters and science . . . I think speculative fiction is very valid, but they forgot the fairy tales.'

While *2001* contained only 35 types of special effects, *Star Wars* is said to have used some 363. In doing so, it has become a fully realized picture of space travel, heretofore limited to the minds of science fiction writers and fans. Interestingly, *Star Wars* was made for less money than *2001* despite the increased number of effects. Lucas and his effects master, John Dykstra, made use of an ingenious computer-controlled animation camera to shoot the extensive footage of model spacecraft, saving costs with an automated photographic process. The final effects are exciting but slightly below the par of those in *2001*, which were slowly created by manual processes at great expense.

*Star Wars* perhaps for the first time put the visual excitement of the science fiction cinema together with an action-filled plot, with great success. The resulting picture was an all-time, record-setting smash hit, grossing $800 million at the box office, and scooping up almost as much through sales of related merchandise. The record album of the score alone brought in $20 million.

*Opposite top :* Luke Skywalker with his laser sword—the force is with him.

*Opposite bottom :* Special effects men sometimes steal the picture from the actors with their fantastic machinery.

*Left :* *Star Wars* (1977). Here Luke Skywalker (Mark Hamill, front seat, left) and Ben (Obi-Wan) Kenobi (Alec Guinness, front seat, right) are stopped for interrogation by enemy troopers. In the back seat are the robots C3PO (left) and R2D2.

*Bottom :* The *Star Wars* crew preparing to blast off. Left to right: Chewbacca, Luke Skywalker (Mark Hamill), Ben (Obi-Wan) Kenobi (Alec Guinness) and Han Solo (Harrison Ford).

Needless to say, such success prompted sequels and imitations. Lucas plans a total of nine *Star Wars* pictures: three cycles of three films each. The first sequel, *The Empire Strikes Back*, released in 1980 and featuring virtually the same cast as the original picture, picked up the adventures of Princess Leia's rebel organization where *Star Wars* left off. The picture is equally fantastic in terms of visual effects and plot, though the story ends on a somber note. The Empire has regained its crushing stance against the rebels, and we find out that Darth Vader's past is uncomfortably linked with Luke Skywalker's. Busy with his Lucas film empire, Lucas left producer Gary Kurtz and director Irvin Kershner to do the honors with *Empire*, though still offering creative input. The third *Star Wars* sequel, *Return of the Jedi*, was released in 1983.

The same year, 1977, brought another success story, though on a smaller scale. Columbia released *Close Encounters of the Third Kind*, written and directed by Steven Spielberg. The story, which doesn't really get off the ground until the last hour, concerns a number of citizens from Indiana who are experiencing strange UFO phenomena, along with others around the country. A documentary-style examination of several incidents is finally tied together when various groups are driven to gather at a mountain in Wyoming by some inexplicable urge. Among them are scientists who have been trying to decode various musical notes which have been recorded from passing UFOs. Gathering at the mountain with devices intended to communicate with intelligent aliens, they welcome several smaller spacecraft and one giant, quarter-mile-wide mother ship. Musical tones are exchanged, and after any suggestion of ill-meaning has been put aside, the Earth people receive their first close contact with extraterrestrial

*Opposite top:* Everyone thinks of Christopher Reeve as Superman. But before him was George Reeves. With that last name, they could have been related. Here he is in the early days in *Superman and the Mole Men* (1951). He went on to play the part on television. Oddly enough, he made his film debut as one of the Tarleton twins in *Gone With The Wind* (1939).

*Opposite bottom:* A scene on Krypton, just before the future Man of Steel is to be rocketed to Earth. The baby's fond parents (Marlon Brando and Susannah York) look on. *Superman* (1978).

*Below:* Luke Skywalker, played by Mark Hamill, riding a Tauntaun, one of the creatures on the ice planet Hoth in *The Empire Strikes Back* (1980).

life. Not only is a missing Earth child dropped off, but so are hundreds of pilots and seamen lost in the Bermuda Triangle over the years.

*Close Encounters of the Third Kind* is more of a religious film dealing with the nature of superhuman beings than it is a science fiction film. Its highly mystical, speculative content has drawn both sharp criticism from those who call it 'anti-science', and praise from those who call it a pioneering attempt to visualize answers to the biggest of questions. Isaac Asimov called the film an influence capable of leading audiences away from rationalism and toward mysticism. Ray Bradbury, an equally respected science fiction author, dubbed it 'the greatest film of our time'.

The film boasts spectacular special effects. Douglas Trumbull, who had worked on *2001*, *The Andromeda Strain* and his own science fiction film, *Silent Running*, was asked to create images of UFOs that would meet any number of abstract, subjective definitions, yet give an appearance of power and motion. The brilliantly lit craft, especially the immense mother ship, are most impressive—worth the $3.5 million tab. Performances by Richard Dreyfuss, Melinda Dillon and Francois Truffaut are less convincing. The actors appear as confused about their roles as do their characters about having to make contact with extraterrestrials.

Three films following these science fiction blockbusters were *Superman* and *Superman II* and *III*, released in 1978, 1981, and 1983. All are marginally science fiction in content; the scene on Superman's home planet, Krypton, in the original film, is closest to it. But all were able to capitalize on the increased public acceptance of science fiction and fantasy themes owing to the popularity of *Star Wars*. The brilliant acting of Christopher Reeve as the hero somehow saves the films from muddled writing and occasionally flimsy special effects.

One film that was almost guaranteed to recoup its investment from *Star Trek* fans alone was *Star Trek: The Motion Picture*, directed by Robert Wise and released by Paramount in 1979. Much of the television series' original cast, including William Shatner, Leonard Nimoy, De Forest Kelley and other crew members of the starship *Enterprise*, were reunited for what amounts to no more than another of their episodes of meeting an alien life form.

The film had both special effects superpowers, John Dykstra and Douglas Trumbull, on its side; indeed, the effects are top-quality, especially an innovative visualization of entering 'warp,' or hyper-light speeds. But the film was otherwise a disappointment to many fans expecting more than the usual romp through space with Kirk and the gang.

Mostly at fault was Paramount, which couldn't decide whether the project, committed to for several years, should take the form of a television series, a made-for-television movie or a full-blown feature film. The project was handed over to more than a dozen writers, and with each script rejection, the powers-that-were became less sure of what they wanted. Finally, the studio plucked the pilot episode of a rejected revival television series, and threw it together before the public could lose its taste for science fiction. The result wasn't what *Star Trek*'s creator Gene Roddenberry wanted, exactly, but once the material was chosen, director Wise and the cast did an excellent job of restoring some professionalism to the project.

Another 1979 science fiction film knew its target exactly: the cold, calculated terror of *Alien*, released by Fox. Dan O'Bannon, who had started his career with *Dark Star*, directed the story about a human space crew on a galactic expedition who find the ruins of an old spacecraft built by aliens. One of the creatures somehow comes to life. It has the terrifying ability to reproduce by entering the bodies of living organisms. The rest of the film is a suspenseful battle between the crew and the alien for control of their ship.

While *Alien*'s special effects and cool direction are superb, what may have insured its spectacular box-office success was a huge media-blitz ad campaign featuring the clever slogan, 'In space, no one can hear you scream,' which all of America was exposed to. Science fiction had arrived at the era of super-hype; virtually any picture, no matter how bad, can gross millions if turned into a media showpiece. Fortunately, *Alien* is chillingly good.

Perhaps if the Disney studio had launched a more spectacular campaign for its 1979 *The Black Hole* that picture might have done better. Gary Nelson directed the space epic about the crew of the Palomino, an exploratory

*Left :* Christopher Reeve in the title role of *Superman* (1978), straightening the tracks so that the train won't be derailed.

*Opposite below :* The 1970s closed with *Alien* (1979), a moody piece that fascinated some audiences, and, with its vicious lizardlike creature raising havoc aboard a space vehicle, turned the stomachs of others. Aside from the repulsive intruder, the picture featured the plot twist of having one of the personnel aboard the spacecraft turn out to be a robot.

*Below :* The cast photograph for *Star Trek—The Motion Picture* (1979).

spaceship, who run into a sort of space-bound Captain Nemo and his huge, ornate ship Cygnus. They discover that the villain, Dr Hans Reinhardt (Maximilian Schell) is up to no good, having turned most of the Cygnus' crew into mindless slaves. He'd like to do the same to several of the visitors, and has a menacing robot named Maximilian to help carry out such deeds. After finding out these dark secrets, struggling against Reinhardt, and in the process destroying the Cygnus, the visitors begin to slip into the neighboring black hole, a 'tear in the fabric of space' beyond which lies mystery. Like so many other ill-fated science fiction films, *The Black Hole* has no real ending; our heroes are sucked into the hole, where a show of lights and camera effects vaguely suggests some sort of transformation of the crew into a different level of existence. It's entirely a religious, not scientific, ending.

The acting by Yvette Mimieux, Robert Forster, Ernest Borgnine and Joseph Bottoms was extremely inconspicuous compared to the film's spectacular, if misguided, special effects. *The Black Hole*'s distinguished special effects team created an incredible variety of illusions,

*Above :* Malcolm McDowell as H G Wells riding his time machine in *Time After Time* (1979). The plot is fun, but rather complicated. Wells follows Jack the Ripper to present-day San Francisco, captures him, sends him to the outer spheres of the galaxy, and takes the modern young woman he has fallen in love with back to Victorian England with him.

*Opposite top :* Workers fill their oxygen tanks on Con-Am 27, a mining complex on Io, a volcanic moon of Jupiter, in the suspenseful film *Outland* (1981).

*Opposite bottom :* Everett McGill as a courageous warrior who ventured into the vast uncharted world of the Ice Age in search of the life-sustaining element in *Quest for Fire* (1982).

including 10 times as many matté shots as those in *Star Wars* and a fascinating black hole illusion.

A much more interesting story was to be had in *Time After Time*, from Warner, 1979. Malcolm McDowell starred as the young H G Wells who travels forward in time to modern San Francisco in his famous time machine, only to find that Jack the Ripper has used the machine to evade capture. Mary Steenburgen also starred in this exciting time-chase, directed by Nicholas Meyer and featuring the special effects of Larry Fuentes and Jim Blount.

The next big-budget science fiction picture, inspired largely by *Alien*'s high-technology look, was *Outland*, written and directed by Peter Hyams in 1981. Sean Connery, the screen's former James Bond, starred as a Federal space marshal sent out to Io, one of Jupiter's moons, to clean up the act of a boisterous mining colony. The management, lead by Peter Boyle, has been involved in the sale of a dangerous amphetamine which increases worker productivity—but also causes lethal bursts of violence.

After the set-up *Outland* has the same plot as the Western classic, *High Noon*; Connery's pleas for help from the inhabitants are ignored, and he must face Boyle's team of henchmen single-handedly. As an audience, we are somewhat disappointed at the end, when after a suspenseful chase and showdown, all Connery does to show his vengeance is punch Boyle in the nose. This does not seem to be enough gut feeling for him to have put so much at stake in the first place, considering his wife and child have walked out on him.

Otherwise, the film is exciting, and the sets, designed by Philip Harrison, are 'high-tech' design brought to its ultimate use. The colony is a twisting, dark, grimy mass of steel girders and plastics. Noteworthy as the marshal's only friend is a middle-aged woman doctor, played with humor by Frances Sternhagen, *Outland*'s comic relief.

Most recently created, taking the cue from the opening scenes of *2001*, is Jean-Jacques Annaud's *Quest for Fire*, released in 1982. The film attempts to show prehistoric man's attempts to control fire, a tool which, the film's characters realize, offers them defense against darkness and its dangers as well as a means of cooking meat.

The film is important for its characterization of these primitive men as more than just intelligent animals. It shows what early man likely exhibited that set him apart from the apes: an intellectual curiosity, the capacity for a range of emotions, the ability to communicate complex thoughts to others and to show sensitivity toward them. Significantly, the film gives the cinema its first impression of prehistoric love and sex.

More importantly, *Quest for Fire*, released by Fox, illustrates that major Hollywood studios have retained their ability to treat science fiction seriously, though not often enough. Even after landmark films like *2001*, there is plenty of room for innovation in the science fiction cinema.

For those who enjoy everything science fiction films have to offer, there is much to look forward to.

# The Stars

*Above :* Buster Crabbe as *Buck Rogers* (1939).
*Left :* Christopher Reeve as *Superman* (1978).

T he science fiction cinema is unlike any other genre in that it has created few, if any, actual 'stars'. If you ask someone, 'Name a few science fiction movie stars of the past', you will likely encounter bewilderment. An ardent fan would point out Buster Crabbe of the *Flash Gordon* serials, and Charlton Heston, who appeared in several science fiction films during the 60s and 70s. Those are the only two who have made a substantial number of science fiction films for any one period of time.

But many actors have become associated with their science fiction roles, regardless of whether the role in which they appeared was their screen debut, from which they went on to stardom in other films, or whether it was the pinnacle of their careers.

Let's take a look at those actors who made a memorable

contribution to the science fiction cinema. And, since it is most often the filmmaking, not the acting, that steals the show in great science fiction movies, we should take this opportunity to find out more about some of the finest directors, too.

## Connery, Sean (Scotland, 1930–    )

After an unlikely combination of navy training and some stage acting experience, Connery made his screen debut in 1956, and since has appeared in numerous fantasy and science fiction films. The most famous of them, of course, are the James Bond films; his appearance in them ranged from 1962's *Dr No* to *Diamonds Are Forever* of 1971, a total of six films. His rugged appearance and honest demeanor make him the ideal film hero. Selected credits: *No Road Back* (1956); *Darby O'Gill and the Little People* (1960), a Disney affair; *Zardoz* (1974); *Outland* (1981).

## Heston, Charlton (US, 1924–   )

Perhaps the epitome of the modern screen hero, Heston began his film stardom with De Mille's *The Greatest Show On Earth* as a darkly motivated ringmaster. He has appeared in a number of religious and historical epics, often as a glamour-boy gladiator; ironically, the use of his presence as 'beefcake' sometimes offended his sensibilities as a Hollywood family man. Heston first studied drama at Northwestern University, and in the late 40s received roles in productions of the classics on CBS live teleplays. He has made a large number of films of dubious quality in the past fifteen years, in each one taking up the standard square-jawed hero-on-his-own role. Selected credits: *Dark City* (1950); *Ben Hur* (1959); *Planet of the Apes* (1968); *The Omega Man* (1971); *Soylent Green* (1973); *Earthquake* (1974).

## Mason, James (Great Britain, 1909–    )

An actor of outstanding talent and versatility, Mason was educated as an architect before a brief shot at the theater. After his debut in film, he became the most suave leading man on Britain's silver screen of the 30s. His popularity increased during the war years, and he played an amazing range of roles, from fiendish villains to sensual lovers, in films varying from camp to moody suspense thrillers. He was particularly adept at playing spies and military men, and portrayed Rommel twice. He is as appealing today as he was in the 30s for his distinguished, intelligent presence on the screen. Selected credits: *Late Extra* (1935); *The Man in Grey* (1943); perhaps his best performance in *Odd Man Out* (1947); *20,000 Leagues Under the Sea* (1954); *Journey to the Center of the Earth* (1959); *Frankenstein: The True Story* (1973); *The Boys From Brazil* (1980).

68

*Top:* Charlton Heston in *The Omega Man* (1971).

*Above:* Leonard Nimoy as Dr Spock in *Star Trek—The Motion Picture* (1979).

*Right:* Sean Connery in *Zardoz* (1974).

## Massey, Raymond (Canada, 1896–1983)

Originally an actor on the English stage, Massey lent his forboding height and deep, resonant voice to his debut role as Sherlock Holmes in Jack Raymond's 1931 *The Speckled Band*. His commanding appearance in the science fiction classic *Things to Come*, 1936, gave strength to the film's otherwise uneven acting. The same attributes landed him the title role in *Abraham Lincoln in Illinois*, 1939, for which he is most remembered. Eventually, Massey enjoyed a starring role as Dr Gillespie in the 'Dr Kildare' television series of the early 1960s. He has delivered a great many strong supporting performances as well as an occasional lead during his long career. Selected credits: *The Fountainhead* (1949); *East of Eden* (1955) opposite James Dean.

## Nimoy, Leonard (US, 1931–    )

Nimoy's contribution toward popularizing science fiction with his television character, 'Mr Spock', is virtually incalculable. The series *Star Trek* was a forum for some of the most intelligent science fiction film presented during the 60s, and the intriguing Vulcan provided many an interesting study of psychology and the struggle of emotion vs logic. Nimoy was born and educated in Boston, a drama scholar at Boston College, and spent several years playing small parts in Hollywood and on television before landing the *Star Trek* role. Nimoy is a dignified and talented actor who has said he very much enjoys the Spock role, though he has diversified with the writing of several poetry books, including 1975's *I Am Not Spock*. Having returned to motion pictures with the current *Star Trek* sequels, Nimoy has recently appeared in the remake of a science fiction classic and as host of television's *In Search Of*. Selected credits: *Seven Days in May* (1964); *Invasion of the Body Snatchers* (1978).

## Peck, Gregory (US, 1916–    )

A distinguished actor who lent respectability to two science fiction films, *On the Beach* and *The Boys from Brazil*, Peck's good looks and appropriateness for decent protagonist roles have rendered him a star from the beginning, and few films in which he has appeared have flopped. Peck has also produced several films, and has gained a reputation as a political figure for his outspoken liberalism. Selected credits: debut in *Days of Glory* (1944); *Gentleman's Agreement* (1947); *On The Beach* (1959); *To Kill A Mockingbird* (1963); *The Boys from Brazil* (1980).

## Pidgeon, Walter (Canada, 1897–    )

Mentioned here for his memorable role as Morbius in *Forbidden Planet* of 1956, Pidgeon was a skilled character actor from the days of the silent films who led a successful career but was lacking in the charisma found in box-office idols. As a contract player for MGM from 1937 on, Pidgeon most often played what he was: a loyal, competent team-player type. However, he lent the screen some of its best villain performances from time to time, and received top billing in many 'B' films. Selected credits: *The Gorilla* (1931); *The Kiss Before the Mirror*, for director James Whale in 1933; Nick Carter in *Nick Carter, Master Detective* (1939). Pidgeon has rounded out his career playing mature, conservative types in numerous films, most recently some of the disaster genre.

## Rains, Claude (Great Britain, 1889–1967)

Known for a career based largely on fine character acting, Rains was a slight, sophisticated type who often played professionals, but also gave a cool, calculating edge to the villains he played. Fondly remembered for his debut in 1933's *The Invisible Man*, Rains made a number of films later on for Frank Capra and Michael Curtiz. After leaving Hollywood in 1956 for the stage, Rains made a few more films before his death. Selected credits: Prince John in *The Adventures of Robin Hood* (1938); Senator Payne in Capra's *Mr. Smith Goes to Washington* (1939); police chief in *Casablanca* (1943); Nazi spy opposite Ingrid Bergman in Hitchcock's *Notorious* (1946); *Lost World* (1960); *Twilight of Honor* (1963).

## Rennie, Michael (Great Britain, 1909–1971)

Included here for his understated performance as Klaatu the alien in Robert Wise's *The Day the Earth Stood Still*, opposite Patricia Neal in 1951. Selected credits: *Lost World* (1960); *Cyborg 2087* (1966).

## Robertson, Cliff (US, 1925–    )

Significant as the only actor ever to receive an Oscar award for lead actor in a science fiction film (*Charly*), Robertson was born the son of a wealthy California rancher and studied at the Actor's Studio after serving in the Navy during World War II. Robertson played regularly on Broadway throughout the 50s, notably in *Mr Roberts* from 1948–1950. After several promising performances as sensitive, innocent types in that decade, his career turned downward somewhat. He was so interested in the role of Charly in *Flowers For Algernon* that he formed his own production company so that he could star in the film version. His other most memorable role was John Kennedy in *PT 109* (1963). Selected credits: *Picnic* (1956); opposite Joan Crawford in *Autumn Leaves* (1956), directed by Robert Aldrich; *The Naked and the Dead* (1958); *The Best Man* (1964); *Charly* (1968).

## Sellers, Peter (Great Britain, 1925–1980)

Sellers' versatility was displayed in Stanley Kubrick's science fiction satire, *Dr Strangelove*, in 1963. A gifted

*Above :* William Shatner as Admiral Kirk of *Star Trek* fame.

*Left :* Peter Sellers as President Muffley in *Dr Strangelove.*

*Below :* A scene from *20,000 Leagues Under the Sea* (1954), directed by Richard Fleischer.

comic writer and actor, Sellers became famous during his run on the long-popular English comedy radio shows, *Ray's a Laugh* and *The Goon Show*, to which such British comedy as *Monty Python* is owing in part. Sellers appeared in a number of small roles in British comedy and drama films during the 50s, frequently in disguise, but he is best known for his portrayal of the bumbling Inspector Clouseau in *The Pink Panther* of 1963, directed by Blake Edwards, and the many sequels which followed. Though he has been criticized as undisciplined and off-beat, Sellers is nonetheless to be remembered as one of the screen's funniest, cleverest actors. Selected credits: *The Mouse That Roared* (1958); *Dr Strangelove* (1963); *What's New, Pussycat?* (1965); *Being There* (1980).

**Shatner, William** (Canada, 1931–    )

Popular among science fiction fans as Captain Kirk of television's *Star Trek*, Shatner studied at McGill University and participated in a great many youth theater productions in his early acting years. Shatner has an extensive Shakespearean background and has played roles in several of the Stratford Shakespeare Festivals. An actor of Broadway experience as well, Shatner appeared in 1961 in *A Shot in the Dark*, a critical success. Shatner has appeared in numerous films and made-for-television movies, and has appeared occasionally in television series, including *The Barbary Coast* and *Sgt Hooker* on ABC. Selected credits: *The Brothers Karamazov* (1958); *Judgement at Nuremberg* (1961); *Outrage* (1964); *Star Trek : The Motion Picture* (1979).

## Directors

**Arnold, Jack** (US, 1916–    )

After the success of *It Came From Outer Space* (1953), this prolific director teamed with producer William Alland to create a large number of respectable science fiction/horror films, typically for Universal Studios. Significant credits: *Creature from the Black Lagoon* (1954); *Tarantula* (1955); *The Incredible Shrinking Man* (1957); *No Name on the Bullet* (1959); *The Mouse that Roared* (1959); *Bachelor in Paradise* (1961).

**Fleischer, Richard** (US, 1916–    )

The son of animator Max Fleischer, Richard worked in the theater before going to work for RKO in 1942. Eventually, he was to serve as director of many mediocre films at 20th Century Fox, but went on to fame after proving himself a skillful director of the action film. He is particularly known for his lavishly mounted spectacles and interesting science fiction films. Significant credits: *The Narrow Margin* (1951); *The Happy Time* (1952); *20,000 Leagues Under the Sea* (1954); *The Vikings* (1957); *Barabbas* (1962); *Fantastic Voyage* (1966); *Tora! Tora! Tora!* (1970); *Soylent Green* (1973).

**Haskin, Byron** (US, 1899–    )

A photographer from 1922 on, Haskin's early years in the motion picture industry included work on the earliest sound film, 1926's *Don Juan*, and Haskin contributed to the refinement of the sound process. He directed a few films during the 20s, though he did not become an active director until 1947, with his *I Walk Alone*. A science fiction enthusiast whose technical background helped him to utilize special effects in his many adventure films, Haskin was chosen to direct Disney's first all-live-action drama, *Treasure Island*, in 1950. He then began a long and fruitful relationship with George Pal, and directed films right up into the 60s. Significant credits: *War of the Worlds* (1953); *The Naked Jungle* (1954); *From the Earth to the Moon* (1958); *Robinson Crusoe on Mars* (1964); *The Power* (1968).

**Kubrick, Stanley** (US, 1928–    )

The son of a Bronx doctor who had an avid fascination for photography, Kubrick developed the same shutterbug characteristics and went on to become a staff photographer for *Look* magazine. He later became interested in the filming of documentaries, and wrote, directed and produced 1951's *Day of the Flight* for his debut. His habit of carrying out several production roles stuck with him, and he even had to raise capital for his first feature film, *Fear and Desire*, of 1953. Kubrick wrote the screenplay for most of his films in the early years of his career, and also for his successes from 1956–1960, after which he moved to Britain to direct and produce, and again, help to write, his blockbusters of the 60s. He is credited with being one of the most technically advanced of all directors and for establishing standards in special effects processes. Significant credits: *The Killing* (1956); *Paths of Glory* (1958); *Spartacus* (1960); *Lolita* (1962); *Dr Strangelove* (1963); *2001: A Space Odyssey* (1968); *A Clockwork Orange* (1971); *Barry Lyndon* (1975); *The Shining* (1979).

**Lang, Fritz** (Austria, 1890–1976)

Lang was trained as an architect, and for a time eked out a living selling cartoons and caricatures (as Méliès had in his early years) and with work as a graphic artist. After World War I he became a writer of thriller novels, and proceeded to make films with similar themes, his first being *The Spiders* (1919). Lang was offered the position of head of the National Socialist film industry, but refused and left Germany. He emigrated to the US where he continued to direct. Lang is known for being as much a designer as a director who framed his scenes exactly before shooting. Lang's wife, Thea von Harbou, was a writer and occasional collaborator. Significant credits: *Metropolis* (1926); *The Woman in the Moon* (1929); *M* (1932), a thriller.

*Top*: Rotwang, Maria and the robot, from *Metropolis* (1926), directed by Fritz Lang.

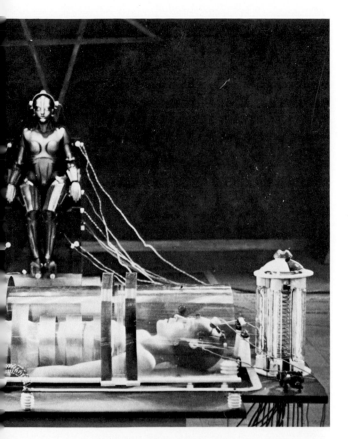

*Above :* Malcolm McDowell confronts his 'droogs' in
*A Clockwork Orange* (1971), directed by Stanley Kubrick.

## Lucas, George (US, 1944–    )

California-born Lucas studied film at the University of Southern California, where in 1967 he produced his first film, *THX-1138*, which won grand prize that year in the National Student Film Contest. The film was later converted to a feature-length release, and Lucas scored financial and critical success with his perceptive and nostalgic *American Graffiti* of 1973. Since then, his greatest accomplishment has been the record-breaking *Star Wars* of 1977. Lucas acted as producer in 1980's *The Empire Strikes Back*, and his film company, Lucasfilm, responsible for the success of *Raiders of the Lost Ark*, is currently at work on further *Star Wars* installments.

## Méliès, Georges (France, 1861–1938)

One of the cinema's pioneers, Méliès brought artistic intent to filmmaking. The son of a wealthy bootmaker, Méliès worked for a time in the family shoe business, but he became interested in magic and left. His parents indulged him with the purchase of Robert Houdin's theater from that famous magician's widow. The theater served as testing ground for Méliès' first films, which contained both theatrical and camera tricks, some of which cannot be explained by experts today. By 1897 he had built the world's first film studio, and shortly thereafter began producing hundreds of short films popular in France and abroad. He failed to grow with the profession, however, and, out of style, returned to the theater in 1913. At the onset of World War I, he declared bankruptcy; the government obtained his theater, and hundreds of his films were burned to salvage war materials. In despair, Méliès burned hundreds more. He ended up a poor candy vendor in the Gare Montparnasse, and lived out his days in a home for impoverished cinema veterans. Fortunately, a cache of many of his films was discovered after his death.

## Pal, George (Hungary, 1908–1980)

Pal began his career as an animator in Budapest, moving to Germany in 1931 and later to Paris, where he produced advertising films featuring his three dimensional characters, the Puppetoons—these sold well in Holland and Britain as well until the War broke out. He then moved to the US in order to compete with Disney in the short films area, winning a special Academy Award in 1943 for process animation combining live actors with animation. He later applied his skills with special effects as the creator of some of the best science fiction films of the 50s, which he most often produced, hiring a director and buying existing science fiction properties for scripts. The director was often Byron Haskin. Pal's films received numerous awards for special effects, but his career petered out in his last 20 years, marked only by a few films with interesting animated effects. Significant productions: *Destination Moon* (1950); *When Worlds Collide* (1951); *War of the Worlds* (1953); *tom thumb* (1958, also directed); *The Time Machine* (1960, also directed).

### Siegel, Don (US, 1912–    )

Siegel first attracted popular attention with such short films as *Hitler Lives* in 1945 and *The Verdict* a year later, which was his first Hollywood feature. He developed a talent for portraying cold violence in films such as 1954's *Riot in Cell Block Eleven* and, more recently, *Dirty Harry* (1971). He is probably best remembered, however, for his chilling *Invasion of the Body Snatchers* of 1956.

### Whale, James (Great Britain, 1896–1957)

Following World War I, Whale started his career as a stage producer in London and later on Broadway, and is credited with R C Sherrif's *Journey's End*, the success of which attracted attention in Hollywood. There he directed the film version of the same play in 1930, though his talents were best displayed in *Frankenstein* in 1931, and the science fiction classic, *The Invisible Man*, of 1933. Whale also directed comedies, gangster epics and musicals, but the quality and popularity of his films declined in his later years. Significant credits: *Kiss Before the Mirror* (1933); *One More River* (1934); *Show Boat* (1936); *The Man in the Iron Mask* (1939).

### Wilcox, Fred McLeod (US, 1908–1964)

After fifteen years in studio publicity work, and as an assistant to director King Vidor, Wilcox began directing both Elizabeth Taylor and Lassie (comparison not intended) in a number of popular films during the 40s. Considering his moderate success directing mild romances and dog adventures, his adept handling of the spectacular *Forbidden Planet* of 1956, comes as something of a surprise. Other significant credits: *Lassie Come Home* (1943); *The Courage of Lassie* (1946); *Hills of Home*.

### Wise, Robert (US, 1914–    )

This widely acclaimed director began in RKO's film editing department in 1933, and gained sufficient mastery of that craft to edit Orson Welles' *Citizen Kane* in 1940 and *The Magnificent Ambersons* in 1942. His first directorial assignment was 1944's *The Curse of the Cat People*, a dark, chilling drama co-directed with Gunther Fritsch. Wise has since directed almost every sort of motion picture; his list of credits is impressive in both variety and overall quality. Significant credits: *Mademoiselle Fifi* (1944); *The Set Up* (1949); *The Day the Earth Stood Still* (1951); *House on Telegraph Hill* (1951); *Desert Rats* (1952); *Executive Suite* (1954); *West Side Story* (1961); *The Sound of Music* (1965); *The Andromeda Strain* (1971); *Star Trek: The Motion Picture* (1979).

*Top:* Gene Barry and Ann Robinson survey the damage in *War of The Worlds* (1963), directed by Byron Haskin.

*Above:* In Georges Méliès' *A Trip to the Moon* (1902), the rocket ship lands in the eye of the Man in the Moon.

*Top:* In *Buck Rogers* (1979), Buck (Gil Gerard) and his robot Twiki are banished to the primitive world of Anarchia.

*Above:* Gene Barry (right) being congratulated for saving the world in *The War of the Worlds* (1963).

# Filmography

Key: D = director S = stars

### Aelita: The Revolt of the Robots
1924, USSR (Mezrabom). D: Yakov Protazanov. S: Nikolai M. Zeretelli, J. Solnzeva.

### Alien
1979 (Fox). D: Dan O'Bannon. S: Sigourney Weaver, Tom Skerritt, Veronica Cartwright, Harry Dean Stanton, John Hurt, Ian Holm.

### The Airship Destroyer
(also known as *Battle in the Clouds*, *Aerial Torpedo*, *Aerial Warfare*, many others), 1909, Great Britain. D: Walter Booth.

### The Andromeda Strain
1971 (Universal). D: Robert Wise. S: Arthur Hill, David Wayne, James Olson, Kate Reid, Paula Kelly.

### The Beast from 20,000 Fathoms
1953 (Warner). D: Eugene Lourie. S: Paul Christian, Paula Raymond, Kenneth Tobey.

### The Black Hole
1979 (Walt Disney Productions). D: Gary Nelson. S: Maximilian Schell, Anthony Perkins, Robert Forster, Yvette Mimieux, Joseph Bottoms, Ernest Borgnine.

### Buck Rogers
1939 (Universal). D: Ford Beebe, Saul A Goodkind. S: Buster Crabbe, Constance Moore, C Montague Shaw, Jack Moran. 12 parts.

### The Cabinet of Dr Caligari (Das Kabinett des Dr Caligari)
1919, Germany (Decla-Bioscop; 1921, MGM). D: Robert Wiene. S: Conrad Veidt, Werner Krauss.

### Charly
1968 (Cinerama). D: Ralph Nelson. S: Cliff Robertson, Claire Bloom.

### A Clockwork Orange
1971, Great Britain (Warner/Polaris). D: Stanley Kubrick. S: Malcolm McDowell, Michael Bates, Adrienne Corri, Patrick Magee.

### Close Encounters of the Third Kind
1977 (Columbia/EMI). D: Steven Spielberg. S: Richard Dreyfuss, Francois Truffaut, Teri Garr, Melinda Dillon, Carey Guffey.

### Dark Star
1972 (University of Southern California; feature release in 1974). D: John Carpenter. S: Dan O'Bannon, USC Drama Dept. students.

## The Day the Earth Stood Still
1951 (United Artists). D: Robert Wise. S: Michael Rennie, Patricia Neal, Hugh Marlowe, Sam Jaffe, Billy Gray.

## Destination Moon
1950 (Eagle-Lion). D: Irving Pichel. S: Warner Anderson, John Archer, Tome Powers, Dick Wesson.

## Dr Strangelove, or, How I Learned to Stop Worrying and Love the Bomb
1963, Great Britain/US (Columbia). D: Stanley Kubrick. S: Peter Sellers, George C Scott, Peter Bull, Sterling Hayden, Keenan Wynn, Slim Pickens.

## The Dog Factory
1904 (Edison). D: Edwin S Porter.

## The Empire Strikes Back
1980 (Fox). D: Irvin Kershner. S: Mark Hamill, Carrie Fishers, Harrison Ford, Anthony Daniels, Kenny Baker, David Prowse.

## FP 1 Does Not Answer (FP 1 Antwortet Nicht)
1932, Germany (UFA). D: Karl Hartl. S: Conrad Veidt, Leslie Fenton.

## Fahrenheit 451
1966, Great Britain (Universal). D: Francois Truffaut. S: Oskar Werner, Julie Christie.

## Fantastic Voyage
1966 (Fox). D: Richard Fleischer. S: Stephen Boyd, Raquel Welch, Edmund O'Brien, Donald Pleasance, Arthur Kennedy.

## Flash Gordon
1936 (Universal). D: Frederick Stephani. S: Buster Crabbe, Frank Shannon, Jean Rogers, Charles Middleton. 13 parts.

## Flash Gordon Conquers the Universe
1940 (Universal). D: Ford Beebe, Ray Taylor. S: Buster Crabbe, Anne Gwynne, Charles Middleton, Frank Shannon. 12 parts.

## Flash Gordon's Trip to Mars
1938 (Universal). D: Ford Beebe, Roger F Hill. S: (Same as above entry). 15 parts.

## Forbidden Planet
1956 (MGM). D: Fred McLeod Wilcox. S: Walter Pidgeon, Anne Francis, Leslie Nielsen, Warren Stevens, Earl Holliman.

## Fun in a Butcher Shop
1901 (Edison). D: Edwin S Porter.

## Futureworld
1976 (American International). D: Richard T Heffron. S: Peter Fonda, Blythe Danner.

## Homunculus the Leader (Homunkulus der Führer)
1916, Germany (Bisoscop). D: Otto Rippert. S: Olaf

*Top:* A scene from a remake of *Flash Gordon*.

*Above:* A long shot of the airborne train with its submarine cargo from Georges Méliès' *The Impossible Voyage/Le Voyage a Travers l'Impossible* (1904).

Fonss, Friedrich Kuhne. Six parts.

**The Impossible Voyage (Le Voyage á Travers l'Impossible)**
1904, France (Star Film Co.). D: George Méliès.

**The Incredible Shrinking Man**
1957 (Universal). D: Jack Arnold. S: Grant Williams, Randy Stuart.

**Invasion of the Body Snatchers**
1956 (Allied Artists). D: Don Siegel. S: Kevin McCarthy, Dana Wynter, King Donovan, Carolyn Jones.

**The Invisible Man**
1933 (Universal). D: James Whale. S: Claude Rains, Gloria Stuart.

**The Invisible Ray**
1936 (Universal). D: Lambert Hillyer. S: Boris Karloff, Bela Lugosi, Frances Drake, Beulah Bondi.

**The Island of Lost Souls**
1932 (Paramount). D: Erle C Kenton. S: Charles Laughton, Bela Lugosi, Richard Arlen, Kathleen Burke.

**It Came from Outer Space**
1953 (Universal). D: Jack Arnold. S: Richard Carlson, Barbara Rush.

**Just Imagine**
1930 (Fox). D: David Butler. S: El Brendel, Frank Albertson, Maureen O'Hara, John Garrick, Marjorie White, Mischa Auer.

**Logan's Run**
1976 (MGM). D: Michael Anderson. S: Michael York, Richard Jordan, Jenny Agutter, Roscoe Lee Brown, Farrah Fawcett-Majors, Peter Ustinov.

**The Lost World**
1925 (First National). D: Harry Hoyt. S: Wallace Beery, Bessie Love, Lewis Stone, Lloyd Hughes.

**The Madness of Dr Tube (La Folie du Docteur Tube)**
1914, France. D: Abel Gance.

**Making Sausages (The End of All Things)**
1897, Great Britain. D: George Smith.

**Master of the World**
1961 (American International/Alta Vista). D: William Witney. S: Vincent Price, Charles Bronson, Henry Hull.

**Marooned**
1969 (Columbia). D: John Sturges. S: Gregory Peck, Richard Crenna, David Janssen, James Franciscus, Gene Hackman, Lee Grant.

**Metropolis**
1926, Germany (UFA). D: Fritz Lang. S: Brigitte Helm, Alfred Abel, Gustav Frohlich, Rudolph Klein-Rogge.

*Top :* Computer-tracking an escapee who has passed his 30th birthday and doesn't want to be exterminated as the law requires in *Logan's Run* (1976).

*Above :* One of the buildings of the future—*Metropolis* (1926).

**The Omega Man**
1971 (Warner). D: Boris Sagal. S: Charlton Heston,
Rosalind Cash, Anthony Zerbe.

**On the Beach**
1959 (United Artists). D: Stanley Kramer. S: Gregory
Peck, Ava Gardner, Fred Astaire, Anthony Perkins.

**Outland**
1981 (Warner Brothers). D: Peter Hyams. S: Sean
Connery, Peter Boyle, Frances Sternhagen.

**Phantom Empire**
1935 (Mascot). D: Otto Brower, B Reeves Eason.
S: Gene Autry, Frankie Darro, Betsy King Ross,
Smiley Burnette. 12 parts.

**Planet of the Apes**
1968, Great Britain (MGM). D: Arthur P Jacobs.
S: Charlton Heston, Roddy McDowall, Kim Hunter,
Maurice Evans, James Whitmore.

**Quest for Fire**
1982 (Fox). D: Jean-Jacques Annaud. S: Everett
McGill, Rae Dawn Chong, Ron Perlman.

**Rocketship X-M**
1950 (Lippert). D: Kurt Newmann. S: Lloyd Bridges,
Hugh O'Brian, Osa Massen, John Emery.

**Rollerball**
1975 (United Artists). D: Norman Jewison. S: James
Caan, John Houseman, Ralph Richardson, Maud Adams.

**The Sausage Machine (Charcuterie Mècanique)**
1897, France. D: Auguste and Louis Lumière.

**Slaughterhouse-Five**
1972 (Universal/Vanadas). D: George Roy Hill.
S: Michael Sachs, Ron Leibman, Eugene Roche,
Valerie Perrine.

**Sleeper**
1973 (United Artists). D: Woody Allen. S: Woody Allen,
Diane Keaton.

**Soylent Green**
1973 (MGM). D: Richard Fleischer. S: Charlton
Heston, Edward G Robinson, Leigh Taylor-Young,
Chuck Connors, Brock Peters, Joseph Cotton.

**Star Trek: The Motion Picture**
1979 (Paramount). D: Robert Wise. S: William Shatner,
Leonard Nimoy, DeForest Kelley, James Doohan,
George Takei, Majel Barrett, Walter Koenig, Nichelle
Nichols, Persis Khambatta, Stephen Collins.

**Star Wars**
1977 (Fox). D: George Lucas. S: Alec Guinness, Mark
Hamill, Carrie Fisher, Harrison Ford, Anthony Daniels,
Kenny Baker, David Prowse.

**The Thing from Another World**
1951 (RKO/Winchester). D: Christian Nyby. S: Robert

*Top:* Everybody's favorite indoor sport—*Rollerball* (1975).
The game was a combination of ice hockey and roller derby.

*Above*: Michael Sachs as Billy Pilgrim, with Valerie Perrine, on the planet Trafalmador in Slaughterhouse-Five (1972).

Cornthwaite, Kenneth Tobey, Margaret Sheridan, James Arness.

### Things to Come
1936, Great Britain (United Artists). D: William Cameron Menzies. S: Raymond Massey, Edward Chapman, Ralph Richardson, Margaretta Scott.

### THX 1138
1971 (Warner/America Zoetrope). D: George Lucas. S: Robert Duvall, Donald Pleasance, Pedro Colley, Maggie McOmie.

### Time After Time
1979 (Warner). D: Nicholas Meyer. S: Malcolm McDowell, Mary Steenburgen, David Warner.

### The Time Machine
1960 (MGM). D: George Pal. S: Rod Taylor, Yvette Mimieux, Alan Young, Sebastian Cabot.

### A Trip to the Moon (Le Voyage dans la Lune)
1902, France (Star Film Company). D: George Méliès. S: Ballerinas of the Théâtre du Châtelet, acrobats of the Folies Bergère.

### The Tunnel (Der Tunnel)
1933, Germany (UFA); also, *Transatlantic Tunnel*, 1935, Great Britain (Gaumont). D: Maurice Elvey. S: Richard Dix, Leslie Banks, Walter Huston.

### 20,000 Leagues Under the Sea
1954 (Buena Vista/Walt Disney Productions). D: Richard Fleischer. S: Kirk Douglas, James Mason, Paul Lukas, Peter Lorre.

### 2001: A Space Odyssey
1968, Great Britain (MGM). D: Stanley Kubrick. S: William Sylvester, Keir Dullea, Gary Lockwood, Douglas Rain.

### Village of the Damned
1960, Great Britain (MGM). D: Wolf Rilla. S: George Sanders, Barbara Shelley, Michael Gwynn, Laurence Naismith, Martin Stephens.

### War of the Worlds
1953 (Paramount). D: Byron Haskin. S: Gene Barry, Ann Robinson, Les Tremayne, Robert Cornthwaite.

### Westworld
1973 (MGM). D: Michael Crichton. S: Yul Brynner, Richard Benjamin, James Brolin.

### When Worlds Collide
1951 (Paramount). D: Rudolph Mate. S: Richard Derr, Barbara Rush.

### The Woman in the Moon (Die Frau im Mond)
1929, Germany (UFA). D: Fritz Lang. S: Gerdus Marus, Willy Fritsch, Fritz Rasp.

### Zardoz
1974 (Fox). D: John Boorman. S: Sean Connery, Charlotte Rampling, John Alderton.

# INDEX

## ACKNOWLEDGMENTS

The author and publisher would like to thank the following people who have helped in the preparation of this book: Abigail Sturges, who designed it; Thomas G Aylesworth, who edited it; John K Crowley, who did the photo research; Cynthia Klein, who prepared the index.

## PICTURE CREDITS

Thomas G Aylesworth: 1, 8, 9, 12, 14, 15, 17, 18–19, 29 (top right and left), 30–31, 33, 34 (top), 40 (top), 43 (top), 46–47, 47, 48 (bottom), 52 (bottom), 69 (bottom).
The Cinema Shop: 74 (top).
Museum of Modern Art: 21–22, 35, 67, 72–73 (top), 74 (bottom), 76 (bottom), 77 (bottom).
National Film Archive: 19, 20–21, 22 (top), 23 (top), 24, 25, 26–27, 29 (bottom), 32 (bottom), 43 (bottom), 50, 51, 52 (top), 54, 73 (bottom), 76 (top).
Jerry Ohlinger's Movie Material Store: 2, 3, 7, 13, 28, 32 (top), 34 (bottom), 36–37, 38, 39, 40 (bottom), 41, 42, 44, 46, 48 (top), 49, 53, 57 (bottom), 60, 61 (bottom), 64, 65, 66–67, 68, 68–69, 70–71, 72–73 (bottom), 74, (top), 77 (top), 78–79.
Bill Yenne: 6–7, 10–11, 27, 55, 56, 57 (top), 58, 59, 61 (top), 62, 63.